the ULTIMATE
HIKING SKILLS
manual

the ULTIMATE
HIKING SKILLS
manual

David and Charles

A DAVID & CHARLES BOOK

Copyright © David & Charles Limited 2006

David & Charles is an F+W Publications Inc. company
4700 East Galbraith Road
Cincinnati, OH 45236

First published in the UK in 2006

Layout and design copyright © David & Charles
Source material courtesy of *Trail* magazine
© Emap Active

A catalogue record for this book is available from the
British Library.

ISBN-13: 978-0-7153-2254-3
ISBN-10: 0-7153-2254-0

Printed in China by SNP Leefung
for David & Charles
Brunel House   Newton Abbot   Devon

Commissioning Editor: Jane Trollope
Designer: Sarah Clark
Desk Editor: Jessica Deacon
Project Editor: Chris Bagshaw
Production Controller: Kelly Smith

Visit our website at www.davidandcharles.co.uk

David & Charles books are available from all
good bookshops; alternatively you can contact
our Orderline on 0870 9908222 or write to us
at FREEPOST EX2 110, D&C Direct, Newton
Abbot, TQ12 4ZZ (no stamp required UK only);
US customers call 800-289-0963 and Canadian
customers call 800-840-5220.

The publishers wish to thank Guy Procter,
Trail editor, and Susan Voss and her team at
Emap Licensing.

Photographic acknowledgments:
Graham Thompson
Tom Bailey
Neil Hepworth
Jeremy Ashcroft
Ashley Cooper
Terry Adby
Alf Alderson
Matthew Roberts

Contents

Foreword

We are lucky in Britain to have a more intimate and varied landscape than most countries. For me, the British hills have a special beauty but are not to be underestimated, as they do have their dangers.

I began my hillwalking and mountaineering on the North Yorkshire Moors and in the Lake District, graduating to bigger, remoter Scottish Hills and the Alps, and Himalya as my experience, skills and knowledge developed.

Hillwalking today is more popular than ever. It even has its own special clothing, equipment and vocabulary. It may even be classed as a sport by some! The hills and wild places are more accessible than ever and the benefits of exercise and fresh air are well recognized. However, the hazards are real and present and not often found in other sports. There is that frisson with danger, which should never be underestimated. It involves visiting remote places not easily reached by the emergency services. A sudden change in the weather can lead to exhaustion, exposure and hypothermia.

There are few rules to hillwalking, but sound personal judgment is essential. There is no substitute for experience and an acquired knowledge of the perils involved in serious, long mountain days. Even the shortest ramble can have dangers, but the idea is to go out and have fun and enjoyment, aware of the risks and how to minimize them.

However competent and confident you are as a hillwalker, the process of gaining new skills never stops. This book, with its up-to-date, easy-to-use design, allows you to dip in and out of various sections and absorb a wealth of information. There is a mass of relevant and detailed knowledge and advice based around colour photographs to enhance your enjoyment of the outdoors. It is an easily readable guide and aide memoire that will help you when you are planning your days out or just being an armchair mountaineer.

You cannot control the unpredictable weather, but you can learn how to be prepared for it. Similarly, minor accidents such as a twisted ankle can have serious consequences, but if you've got the knowledge of what to do in a range of different situations, you will feel more confident, and better enjoy your hillwalking. Learning how to maximize your performance means you will be able to attempt more adventurous walks, opening up greater opportunities for achievement in the hills. Whether you are a casual rambler, a dedicated Wainwright bagger, or Munroeist, you can benefit from the wisdom encapsulated in this book to help you achieve your ambitions.

For all fell walkers and ramblers venturing into the hills, this handbook contains essential knowledge in an easy-to-read, informative style, touching on every topic of walking. This is a book I would have welcomed when I first started hillwalking over 30 years ago.

Enjoy the book, be safe and enjoy the hills.

Alan Hinkes

Why go hillwalking?

There's nothing simpler or more rewarding than being surrounded by the natural world, away from the stresses of everyday life. Shaking off the humdrum of urban existence is a goal for many outdoor pursuits. Hillwalking takes you into an upland world presenting physical challenges as well as scenes of great beauty. It rewards you not just with a sense of achievement, of having been 'out there' among the towering peaks, but also with a fantastic library of recalled scenes – a ptarmigan in a wintry gulley, silver light on a rain-filled tarn, the glimpse of the sun on distant peaks in ranges that stretch to the horizon. These are the images a hillwalker treasures to take back to 'normal life'.

Improve your skills

But do you really need another book on the subject? After all, you've probably been walking since you first clambered out of the pram, and you may feel you have the hang of it by now. It's a fair point – but this handy little volume is offering to bring a little extra knowledge to your days on the hill, making them safer, more comfortable and much more satisfying. A bit of preparation, and the mastery of a few important skills, can go a long way, and will have you patting yourself on the back for making a shrewd investment.

The first section suggests how you can prepare for going out in the hills. There is a fitness improvement regime, and advice about what foods to eat and what gear you should and shouldn't be carrying and wearing. The section on weather in the hills explains how to interpret weather forecasts and includes valuable tips on surviving the most common extremes. The route planning section asks you to examine your motivations as well as helping you fill in a route card.

The second section contains practical instruction from the top outdoors experts, to navigate, deal with emergencies, and generally be safe and proficient in the hills. Digest this advice and you'll be a cut above the average bobble-hatted daytrippers. In addition there are chapters concentrating on walking in winter, and extending your hillwalks to include overnighting in a tent or mountain shelter.

Finally, there's a chance to reflect on the experiences that hillwalking offers, with professional tips and advice on capturing the magic in photographs and guidance on treading lightly in our often fragile upland environments.

But there's no substitute for getting your boots muddy, so spend a few hours reading these pages, then head for the hills and start putting them into practise.

Preparation

Hillwalking is as much in the mind as in the mountains. You have to be prepared, both physically and mentally, for the challenge. In this section we look at the things you can do to make your trips to the hills more enjoyable and safer. That means being fit and healthy – the 12-week programme here will ensure you are both – and equipped with both the right gear and the right knowledge. Another joy of walking in the hills is planning your trip. The hours spent over maps, charts and guidebooks are an integral part of the activity itself. Anticipating the quiet of a high corrie seen first on a map, or recalling the swirls of mist through towering rock architecture on your last trip, form both the motivation and purpose.

Take heed of the advice offered here on route planning and understanding diverse weather patterns and you will enjoy that thrill to the full. But safety should always be foremost in your mind. In the same way as it is foolish to venture into the hills without the physical strength to get you out again, you shouldn't embark on an initial fitness programme without first assessing your existing capacity for exercise. See your doctor if you have any doubts, and don't continue any form of training exercise if you feel pain or abnormal discomfort. You do, after all, want to get to the hills safely in the first place.

Improve your hill fitness

You'll enjoy your walking more if you're physically prepared. This 12-week programme focuses on improving stamina using a range of aerobic activities, building strength with a basic home gym, and increasing flexibility, balance and co-ordination through a series of stretches and exercises. There's even some hillwalking included, too.

All you have to do is make sure you have the right gear: good training shoes, a mat, some hand weights and possibly a heart-rate monitor. At the end of the programme you'll have the strength and stamina to complete a tough scramble during a six-hour expedition, with an overall climb of 1,100m (3,609ft). On completion, try to keep up your activity; all adults should be active for around 30 minutes a day for good health.

Getting started

How do I measure my current fitness?

Before you start your hill-training regime, take a note of your current fitness level by checking your resting heart rate. The simplest way to do this is by placing two fingers (of your left hand) at the side of your Adam's apple – the front knobble in your neck. Count the pulses for 15 seconds against your wristwatch, then multiply by four to calculate your current heart rate per minute. Measure your pulse first thing in the morning before you get out of bed (to find out your resting heart rate) and again just after exercising, to see how much faster it is and how quickly it slows down (this is your recovery rate).

How hard should I be working?

For best results from this programme, you'll need to work at approximately 65–70 per cent of your maximum heart rate (MHR). To work out your MHR, simply subtract your age from 220. So, if you're 36, your theoretical maximum heart rate is 184 beats per minute, and you'll need to check that your pulse stays at an optimum level (between 119–128 beats per minute) during your workout.

How can I tell if I'm getting fitter?

The harder you exercise, the higher your heart rate, which indicates how fast your heart is pumping oxygenated blood to your muscles. Eventually, as your fitness improves, you will be able to achieve a set workload with a lower heart rate, where all other things are equal. Try to keep a record of your resting heart rate in a training diary so you can see how it slows down as you get fitter.

If you haven't been active for a long time, or have any concerns over your health, you should check with your doctor before starting any exercise programme.

Warm-up and stretches

Before you start this sequence of stretches, jog on the spot for a few minutes to gently warm up your muscles. Then, follow the stretches without forcing or bouncing, holding each stretch for 15 seconds. Don't hold your breath and if any of the exercises cause pain, stop immediately and seek medical advice. Repeat each stretch four times to warm up for the strength exercises on pages 17–19, and to improve overall flexibility. Use the same stretches after your workout too.

1 Calf stretch
Stand with one foot forwards, knee bent. Keeping your back knee straight and facing front, lean forwards over your bent knee without bending at the waist and keeping your heel on the floor. You should feel a gentle pull in the calf of the back leg. Hold for a count of 15. Repeat with the other leg.

2 Hamstring stretch
Lie on your back with one knee bent. With both hands support the back of your thigh. Straighten your knee until you feel a gentle stretch at the back of your thigh. Make sure your back is flat on the floor and your chin is tucked into your neck. Hold for a count of 15, then repeat on the other side.

3 Quadriceps and knee stretch
Stand and hold one knee behind you, bringing it up towards your bottom until you feel a gentle stretch. Support your ankle with your hand as you hold the stretch. Make sure the knee of the other leg is slightly bent. Don't lean forwards or allow your back to arch. Hold for a count of 15. Repeat with the other leg.

4 Hip stretch
Stand in a wide walking position. Put both hands on your front thigh and keep the other knee straight. Push your hip forwards and down, keeping your back straight. You should feel the stretch in the front of the hip and in the thigh of the straight leg. Hold for a count of 15 and then repeat with the other leg.

5 Arm stretches
Raise your arm, bending your elbow behind your head with your hand behind your neck (5a). With your other hand, gently pull your elbow towards the opposite side. Keep your elbow bent and behind your head. Don't push your head forward. Hold for a count of 15. Repeat on the other side. Next (5b), stretch one arm over the opposite shoulder by pushing it at the elbow with your other arm. Hold for a count of 15, then repeat on the other side.

Your personal fitness chart

Use the chart on pages 15–16 for week-by-week guidance on which activities will help improve stamina and build strength. The final column shows how you can use hillwalking to put fitness gains into practice. The chart offers scope for variety (so you don't get bored) and is designed to deliver steady progress.

After week two, fitness should start to feel as though it's becoming part of your routine. To stay motivated throughout the 12 weeks, adjust the programme towards your own favourite activities – perhaps mountain biking or squash – and be prepared to swap equivalent exercises around from one week to the next.

Improve stamina

Hillwalking is an 'endurance activity' involving hours of aerobic exercise. All aerobic activities rely on a strong cardiovascular system (heart, lungs and blood vessels) to supply your muscles with oxygen and energy (stored as fat in the body). Use the chart below to choose two aerobic activities each week during the programme, and change them every now and again to keep your interest.

Build strength and balance

As you increase your range of movement, you'll need to strengthen that new range. The exercises on the following pages will improve your strength, muscle tone, co-ordination, flexibility and balance. However, make sure you give your body time to recover after a weights session. As the weeks progress the chart calls for two sessions a week – but make sure they don't fall on two consecutive days.

Developing better balance and co-ordination will help you avoid injury and improve technique on uneven ground. To improve your balance, practise standing on one leg for 30 seconds. Repeat with the other leg. Move your arms to increase the difficulty, and try closing your eyes. Do this as often as you can during the 12-week programme.

Hillwalking practice

Take time to find local routes that match the chart descriptions as closely as possible (in terms of gradient and distance – don't worry if you don't have a loch, forest or sea shore nearby). However, to make sure you're enjoying the programme as much as possible, it's worth planning day trips slightly further afield at the weekend – the change of scenery will help you forget you're trying to get fit!

Before you go hillwalking

- Take time for a proper warm-up before you start – a five-minute walk on the flat where your pace becomes quicker will do – and include stretches as shown on page 13. Cool-down stretches may help to reduce muscle stiffness next day.

Improve stamina	
Choose two activities each week for 20 minutes	
Cycling	road cycling or mountain biking
Walking	start on the flat and walk briskly for a minimum of 40 minutes
Gym	stationary bike, stepper, cross trainer, rowing machine
Running	progress from brisk walking to jog-walking then running
Classes	spinning, aerobics, step, aqua aerobics – progress from beginners' class/low-impact to high-impact
Swimming	lane swimming – any stroke
Squash	or any competitive racquet sport
Soccer	keep active throughout the game
Digging	any vigorous gardening will get the heart rate going

Plus any activities which use the arms and legs, causing the pulse rate to work at a minimum of 65 per cent of your maximum heart rate, for 20 minutes

Week	Improve stamina	Build strength and balance	Hillwalking practice
one	Choose two sessions from the aerobic activity menu (page 14) and work at them for at least 20–30 minutes. If joining a fitness class, select a beginners' or low-impact one, to avoid 'overdoing' it and hurting yourself. Prepare to discover muscles you never knew you had!	Perform all the warm-up stretches on page 13, then choose eight of the 11 exercises shown on pages 17–19 (choose three for the legs; two for the arms; one for the back; one for the stomach) and repeat each exercise 12–15 times (in other words, 12–15 'reps'). Perform the same sequence twice (make two 'sets').	Take one 2–3 hour flat, easy walk around a reservoir or lake.
two	As your new fitness regime begins to become part of your lifestyle, choose another two aerobic activities from the menu, but this week, you should increase the length of time you spend doing them by five minutes.	Do the same set of exercises, but if you found 15 reps too easy, add an extra 1kg to your hand weights (be sure to buy a pair that's the right weight for you). If you only tried 12, increase the number of reps to 15. Again, perform just two sets.	Choose a forest route for your hillwalking this week, and increase the time by 30 minutes.
three	Ring the changes this week by taking one stepping session: choose from a step machine, a step aerobics class, or set the treadmill at the gym on a small incline. If you don't have access to step classes or equipment, use the stairs at every opportunity.	This week, progress to three sets during your weekly session. If you get bored with one of the exercises, change it for an equivalent one, but keep your pulse rate working.	Find a route with undulating ground and a climb of 400m (1,312ft). If you aren't sure how to read a map or use a compass, attend a two-day course on navigation skills for beginners.
four	Your body will have begun to adapt to your training, and you should notice benefits. This week, increase your cardiovascular/aerobic session duration by another five minutes, or increase resistance (eg higher step or steeper incline on the treadmill).	Set time aside for two weights sessions this week (but not on consecutive days). Each time, reduce your workload to only 12 reps, keeping the weights the same as in week three.	Climb 600m (1,968ft) during a three-hour walk on easy paths.
five	Progress to a more difficult cardiovascular/aerobic exercise class this week – a high-impact one – for a minimum of 30 minutes.	Again, have two weights workout sessions, using the same eight basic exercises and weights, but each time, bring the workload back up to 15 reps, for two complete sets.	Walk by the sea where you can climb over low rocks and boulders. Or choose broken track or rougher ground, to improve your balance and co-ordination.
six	Congratulations: you're at the halfway stage! Exercise should feel like a regular part of your weekly routine – which you'd miss! Increase time spent on your cardiovascular/aerobic activities by another five minutes, if possible.	To introduce a little variety and avoid getting bored, this week include two new exercises, bringing your total to ten exercises. Reduce the number of reps back down to 12 to compensate for the extra work.	Select the same route as you did for either week four or five (whichever you found tougher), and increase time by 30 minutes – that is, making the route longer, not taking extra time to do it!

Fitness

15

Week	Improve stamina	Build strength and balance	Hillwalking practice
seven	Make your cardiovascular training more specific to hillwalking, now that your body has better condition. Use a Versa climber machine at the gym, or any equipment that mixes a stepping action with upper arm movement – for stronger scrambling.	This week, focus on improving the quality of the movement of the new exercises. For instance, watch your breathing, and control the speed of your reps.	Walk for four hours on this week's outdoor trek, keeping your height gain to around 600m (1,968ft).
eight	Increase the intensity of each exercise this week, but remember that with more exertion comes more sweat! Drink lots of water. For your aerobic exercise, focus on working at a minimum of 60 per cent of your maximum heart rate for two sessions (see page 12).	This time, increase your workout by making three sets of each of your ten exercises, making only 12 reps. To recap: two workout sessions; ten exercises; 12 reps; three sets. (Pint of beer will taste good after that! Don't forget to do some cool-down stretches.)	This week, plan your route to include an 800m (2,625ft) climb or to take in some rough ground for a four-hour walk.
nine	Make your training more specific to hillwalking, using a light backpack while you're on the stepper or running. Increase your minimum working heart rate to 65 per cent of your maximum.	Try to improve the quality of your movement (form) for the three sets. Look in the mirror as you lift the weights to check stance, and be sure to control the speed of your movements.	Choose a slightly longer route, so that this time you're walking for a minimum of four-and-a-half hours.
ten	Look after your knees this week, using swimming or cycling as one of your cardiovascular aerobic sessions. Opt for a 45-minute gym session to keep activities varied (cadge a guest pass from a friend!).	This week, sneak another few reps into your workout. That is, do two sessions of the ten exercises, making 15 reps in three sets. All that counting should at least take your mind off the pain...	Increase route difficulty with a climb to 1,000m (3,280ft) during a walk lasting a minimum of five hours.
eleven	Use cycling or swimming as a recovery session for the harder hillwalk last week. Take one session of non-weight-bearing activity and one session working at a minimum of 70 per cent of your maximum heart rate.	Keep both sessions the same as last week, but this week focus on movement quality.	Increase walk duration to a minimum of five-and-a-half hours.
twelve	The last week of our fitness programme focuses on improving upper body strength for better scrambling. Take two sessions this week, working at a minimum of 60 per cent of your maximum heart rate to prepare for a strenuous hillwalking session ahead.	Keep both sessions the same as last week, again focusing on movement quality, using the mirror. Keep up your twice-weekly sessions once the programme is over, adding weight or increasing the number of sets and reps in manageable stages.	Select your ultimate long distance, strenuous walk, involving areas of scrambling for six hours with height gain of 1,100m (3,609ft).

- Don't forget to keep your body hydrated with a diluted, low-sugar squash drink as these can be easily absorbed by the body. Eat sandwiches, bananas and carbohydrate snacks such as energy bars, which can be quickly utilized by the body. (If you're watching your weight, choose fruit or sandwiches with a low-fat filling.)

- Always choose routes that suit your ability and fitness, which will progress as you stay with the programme.

Exercises to build your strength

Use these exercises as part of the fitness chart on pages 15–16, after doing the warm-up stretches on page 13.

For the legs

6 Abductor raise
Works: hips (adductors), buttocks (gluteus medius) and outer thighs.
Lie on the floor on your left side with your left leg slightly bent. Use your left hand to support your head and place your right hand in front of you to steady yourself. Keeping your right leg straight and in line with your body, raise it with a slow, controlled movement. Hold for one second, lower, then repeat.

7 Squats with hand weights
Works: legs (quadriceps and hamstrings) and bottom (glutes).
Stand with your feet hip-width apart, a weight in either hand, palms facing inwards. Keeping your chest up, squat down and rise. Your thighs should not go past a 90-degree angle with your knees, and your heels should stay in contact with the ground at all times.

8 Lunges with hand weights
Works: legs (quadriceps and hamstrings) and bottom (glutes).
Hold your weights at your sides with your feet hip-distance apart. Step forward with one leg, bending both knees until your thigh is parallel with your knee. Push back to the starting position. Alternate your legs. Do not let your knee come further forward than your front foot. Do not let your back knee touch the ground.

9 Glutes raise
Works: bottom (glutes) and hamstring.
Support yourself on your elbows and knees with hands together in front of you. Take care to keep your back straight. Keeping your right leg bent raise it into the air. Keep your foot flat and press up into the heel. Count two seconds up and two seconds down.

For the arms

10a   10b

12a   12b

10 Bicep curls with hand weights
Works: front of arms (biceps).

Keep your elbows close to your sides with your palms facing forwards. Pull the weights towards your shoulders, then slowly lower. Ensure you work through the full range of movement. Do not over-extend your elbows. Keep the rest of your body still. Work slowly to control the movement.

12 Tricep extension with hand weights
Works: back of arms (triceps).

Sit upright on a stool or bench with a weight in your right hand behind your head. Extend your arm keeping your elbow close to your head, taking care not to move your elbow. Keep your stomach pulled in and slowly return to the start position. Take four to five seconds to complete the movement.

For the back and shoulders

11a

11b

13a   13b

11 Press-ups
Works: chest and arms (pectorals, deltoids and triceps).

Place your hands directly under your shoulders, keeping your fingers pointing forwards and your legs in line with your body. Lower your body towards the floor without touching it, then push yourself back off the floor to the start position. Do as many as you can.

13 Shoulder press with hand weights
Works: shoulders (trapezius), arms (triceps) and back (deltoids).

Sit on a chair with your back straight and stomach pulled in. With your arms at shoulder height, holding the weights, extend them upwards until they're straight, then return to the starting position. Do not over-extend the elbow.

14a   14b

14   Lateral and frontal raises with hand weights

Works: shoulders (medial deltoid and anterior deltoid).

Lateral raises (left): hold the weights at your sides, palms facing in. Slowly raise your arms to shoulder level and lower. Lead with your elbows and keep your wrists straight.

Frontal raises (right): hold the weight(s) in front of you with your arms down, palms towards you. Raise your arms to the front at shoulder level and lower. Keep your wrists straight.

For the stomach

15a

15b

15   Crunches

Works: stomach (rectus abdominus and transverse abdominus).

Lie on your back bringing your legs up over your hips and cross your ankles. (To make it easier at first, rest your feet against your bottom.) Place your arms either on the front of your thighs, across your chest or beside your head (for the hardest version). Pull your stomach muscles in tight, then slowly curl up, using your abs to lift your shoulders and bottom off the floor at the same time. Don't swing your legs.

16

16   Oblique curls

Works: stomach (internal obliques).

Lie on your back and cross one ankle over the opposite knee. Place your arms either on the front of your thighs, across your chest or beside your head for the hardest version. Pull your abs in tight. Slowly curl up and across, bringing your shoulder towards your opposite bent knee then slowly lower back down. Repeat then change to work opposite side.

Flexibility

These are some of the muscles you will be using with these exercises.

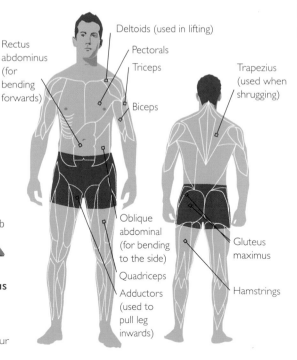

Deltoids (used in lifting)

Rectus abdominus (for bending forwards)

Pectorals

Triceps

Biceps

Trapezius (used when shrugging)

Oblique abdominal (for bending to the side)

Quadriceps

Adductors (used to pull leg inwards)

Gluteus maximus

Hamstrings

Fitness

Flexibility

Test your flexibility

You don't need to be flexible to be a hill-walker, right? Wrong! While you certainly don't need to match the suppleness of a gymnast, the more flexible you are, the less prone to fatigue and injury you'll be. Think about it: the more supple you are, the greater the range of movement your body can comfortably perform without stressing the joints, muscles, tendons and ligaments. Assess your flexibility with this ten-minute test. To prepare, tape a ruler to the floor and grab a pal to record the test result. Now go for a five-minute warm-up walk.

1 Take off your shoes and sit with your legs flat on the floor in front of you with your heels at zero on the ruler. Keep your feet shoulder-width apart for the most accurate result.

2 Hold your arms out in front of you, parallel to the ground, dip your head between them and bend at the waist to smoothly and slowly reach forwards. Breathe out as you stretch.

3 Hold your position at the full extent of the stretch while your mate measures the horizontal distance between your heels and your fingertips in centimetres. Then compare the result with the table below.

1

2

3

Age		Poor	Fair	Good	Excellent	Top dollar!
Teens:	male	under 9cm	9–13cm	14–17cm	18–23cm	over 23cm
	female	under 14cm	14–18cm	19–22cm	23–27cm	over 27cm
20s	male	under 9cm	9–14cm	15–18cm	19–24cm	over 24cm
	female	under 13cm	13–17cm	18–21cm	22–25cm	over 25cm
30s	male	under 8cm	8–12cm	13–17cm	18–22cm	over 22cm
	female	under 12cm	12–16cm	17–20cm	21–25cm	over 25cm
40+	male	under 3cm	3–8cm	9–13cm	14–19cm	over 19cm
	female	under 10cm	10–14cm	15–18cm	19–22cm	over 22cm

Flex your shoulders

Before summer comes and the scrambling season gets under way, increase your shoulder flexibility with this stretch. It's also a useful exercise to do before and after any route where you'll be labouring under a heavy rucksack: by opening the shoulder joints, it'll help you avoid shoulder pain.

Clasp your hands behind your back as shown. Hold the stretch as you take five deep breaths. Swap your hands over and repeat. If you are right-handed, you'll probably find it far easier to clasp your hands together when your right elbow is uppermost (and vice versa if you're left-handed). This shows you just how inflexible your left shoulder is – and why you should therefore fit this stretch into your daily list of chores.

Test your uphill power

The muscles in the front of your thighs – the quads – supply much of the power needed to walk uphill and to brake downhill. Establish the strength of yours with this simple test:

Stand with your back against a wall. Shuffle your feet away from the wall and lower your body until your knee joints are at a 90-degree angle. Your feet must face forwards, directly underneath your knees. Keep the back of your head against the wall and don't put your hands on your legs for support (that's cheating). Time how long you can stay in this position – but be warned, the muscle-burn is harsh.

It's a wise idea to go for a short walk to warm up and cool down your muscles before and after taking this test. Don't try it if you have knee problems.

Less than 15 seconds	**Shocking:** don't plan a speedy ascent of Snowdon just yet – unless it's on the train.
45 seconds	**Could do better:** plan more hills into your weekends and keep the climbs steady.
1 minute 15 seconds	**Okay:** do three sets of 20 squats daily to build up the strength of your quads.
1 minute 45 seconds	**Good:** you should have no trouble tackling some of the classic routes.
2 minutes 15 seconds	**We're impressed:** you sailed through the pain barrier with flying colours.
over 2 minutes 45 seconds	**Top notch:** your quads testify that you're used to pushing yourself to your limits.

Expert's tip

Your calf muscles might be fine while walking, but by the following morning, they may be seized up to the point of agony. How can you avoid the pain?

Stretching really is the best solution to alleviate stiffening muscles. And the most effective time to do it is directly after exercise when your muscles are still warm. You can combine your stretches with the act of removing your boots. First, undo your laces without bending your knees: take your time and you'll feel the stretch in your calves and hamstrings. Next, place one foot on the car bumper with your knee bent: lean forwards over that boot to loosen off your laces and you'll feel the stretch in the calf of your other leg.

Be on your toes!

On steep ascents, it's your calves that take the punishment. But with a little bit of training you can whip them into better shape. Try these calf raises.

Why do them?

The steeper the terrain, the more work your calves have to do. And if you're planning on tackling any snow gullies this winter, you'll need as much calf muscle as you can stuff into a pair of gaiters.

How?

Stand with the balls of your feet on a step and your heels hanging off the edge. Keeping your legs and body straight, raise your heels until you are standing on tiptoe. Hold for two seconds, then slowly lower your heel as far as it will go. Try doing at least 30 of these.

Brain scan

There's more to hillwalking fitness than just physical strength and flexibility. As all hillwalkers know – you often go through a full range of mental states, too, on a long day in the mountains. But what causes these see-saws of mental mood? You have to look at it from your brain's point of view...

Mood

Preparation

1 You start

Commonly the point when people feel the worst. This stage of the walk is the equivalent of a short-intensity workout, which catches the body unawares. Still struggling to adjust to the new level of activity, your brain has not yet started to release inhibitor molecules called endorphins – a natural equivalent of morphine – secreted into the bloodstream by the pituitary gland.

Brain control
Spend five minutes doing gentle stretching exercises before you start to ease your body into the increasing level of activity.

2 You click into gear

At some point during your initial slog, you will experience a second wind. Exercise-induced acidosis of the blood occurs, due to reduced oxygen flow to the muscles. This is detected by the pituitary gland, causing it to release endorphins which bind to pain receptors and suppress discomfort. This results in a state of mild euphoria, making you feel far better about the steepening slope ahead. While endorphin release isn't governed by fitness (you may get your second wind after ten minutes or an hour), if you're out of shape, you may not feel the effects of endorphins at all.

Brain control
Don't be fooled by this release of endorphins: the euphoria will tempt you to speed up your ascent, but it's far better to stick to a comfortable rhythm that you can sustain during the entire ascent.

3 You hit a knife-edge ridge

That flutter in your stomach or the weak feeling in your knees is all down to the hormone adrenalin (or epinephrine, as it is known in more scholarly circles). Released by the adrenal glands on the kidneys, epinephrine attaches itself to receptor sites on your heart, brain, eyes and intestine. It kicks your heartbeat up a notch, dilates your pupils and reduces circulation to your intestine and stomach, leading to that wide-eyed nauseous feeling you get in high places. This allows extra oxygen to be redirected to the limbs, so you may feel agitated, jumpy or unusually energetic. This is known as the 'fight or flight' syndrome. It provides extra energy to the parts of your body that will get you out of harm's way quickly – at the expense of areas that won't immediately aid your escape, such as your digestive system.

Brain control
Your butterfly-filled stomach is a physical result of your brain recognizing the danger, and not because you're a wimp. Take deep, slow breaths to improve oxygen intake.

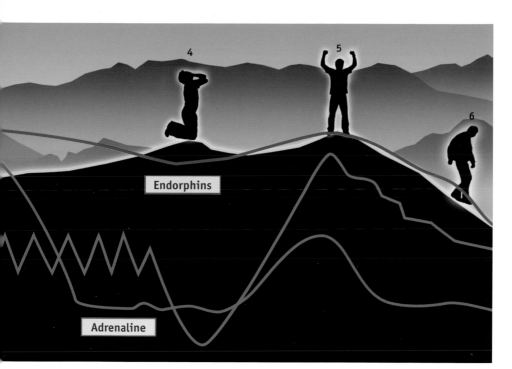

Endorphins

Adrenaline

4 You reach a false summit

The exhaustion that takes hold at a false summit is a balance between physical and psychological fatigue. As you approach a point you believe is the end of your ascent, it's common to increase activity in a final push for the top, in much the same way as an athlete will sprint the last few yards of a race, using up the last of your energy reserve. Discovering the summit lies ahead, up yet more ascent, can cause apathy and fatigue due to your reduced energy levels.

Brain control

Eat a banana. It's not only a good source of slow-release energy; it also contains tryptophan and vitamin B6, which together help your body to produce serotonin, a feel-good chemical that improves your mood.

5 You hit the high point

The euphoria you experience on hitting a summit may not merely be the result of achieving a hard-earned goal, though this does have a lot to do with it. New research has linked this feeling with a substance called phenylethylamine, a chemical naturally produced in the brain that's linked to the regulation of moods during exercise. An enzyme changes the chemical into phenylacetic acid, which has a similar chemical structure to amphetamines and can cross from the blood to the brain. It has been suggested that phenylacetic acid may be linked to the phenomenon known as 'runner's high', a feeling experienced by many top athletes on completion of a race. This may make you think you are ready for another summit due to its seemingly revitalizing effects.

Brain control

Be aware that your brain, awash with chemicals, may trick you into thinking you are less physically tired than you really are. Sit down for five minutes on the summit and have a snack before making any decisions.

6 You descend

The jarring movements of descent are the most stressful on joints, and the endorphin production of the walk's earlier stages slows or even ceases as your heart rate returns to normal-ish levels. This makes you increasingly aware of your aches and pains. The fitter you are, the less you will notice this; but if you are only an occasional summiteer, descent may well be the most uncomfortable part of the walk.

Brain control

Break the descent into several short sections, with a food reward for completing each. This goal-achievement will heighten your mood.

Caring for your knees and feet

The human knee is a troublesome thing, aching, breaking and creaking at the slightest provocation. So where are we going wrong?

Walkers don't often see themselves as sportspeople, but if you're going for an eight-hour walk, you're putting your legs under as much stress as someone who plays squash or goes running a couple of times a week. Women are more prone to biomechanical injuries because their wider hips give them a shifting centre of gravity.

When people first experience knee pain, often they accept it or try to manage it. When it becomes a problem, you might buy a pair of trekking poles. These work, but only to a limited degree. You can help the symptoms improve, but the underlying cause is still there.

The most common knee injuries

Walkers often complain of knee pain on descents, pain in the inside knee or behind the kneecap, and pain in the outside knee (iliotibial band syndrome).

The causes

Everyone has a distinctive gait which becomes more exaggerated as we get older. Very few folk have perfect gait, with the body's weight aligned perfectly through the feet, ankles, knees and hips. Most people have a slight biomechanical imbalance, which your body will compensate for – from the feet upwards – in an attempt to bring the centre of balance back in over the feet. It could be a roll of the foot, a flick of the ankle, or an outward or inward

movement of the knee. However, in some people, there's excessive movement, and it concentrates pressure on a part of the joint that can't carry that kind of load. If your knees hurt, you have to stop the movement and encourage the body to adopt a more neutral position. You can do that with off-the-peg or custom-made orthotics.

Even if it's the jarring of a steep downhill that brings on the symptoms of pain or discomfort, it's only an aggravating factor, not the cause. Most knee injuries relate to excessive movement in the joint, rather than shock transferred through the limb. Cushioning or shock-absorbing insoles can add another kind of movement.

However, orthotics – EVA sport insoles personalized to cradle and lift the foot – fit inside the boot and hold the foot in a more neutral position to control excessive movement. This reduces stress on joints and soft tissues in the legs and lower back. You can buy off-the-peg orthotics or have them fitted by a qualified podiatrist.

Knee injuries caused by a twist, tear or knock will usually repair with a few weeks of rest and rehab. If, however, your injury 'just happened'; if pain worsens with activity, but clears up when you lay off, then you may have a biomechanical problem. This won't just go; it will need specialist attention if you want to stay active. Ask your doctor for advice, or make an appointment with a podiatrist.

Coping with age

It's not inevitable that you'll have aches and pains as you get older! Problems appear because as the body ages, the degree of discrepancy in skeletal misalignment increases: the collagen which makes up tendons and ligaments becomes less resilient, so things are more likely to snap rather than spring back into place. People start to have problems such as fallen arches, which become set in position. It sounds depressing, but the good news is that this process isn't irreversible. Over time the orthotic encourages the ligaments and tendons to stretch back, allowing the foot to adopt a more relaxed neutral position when non-weightbearing, and to be less gnarly. Hill-walking is one of the best ways to stay active in later life, but as you get older you can't take your body for granted.

Make your knees last a lifetime

There are three things you can do to ensure your knees are still in good order when you're climbing hills in your dotage.

First, every time you go out, take it steady for the first five minutes of your walk or ride, and don't burn up the first hill you come to. This will dramatically reduce your chances of sustaining a knee injury.

Second, get into the habit of stretching your hamstring, Achilles and quads afterwards. This stops the leg muscles from contracting and shortening after exercise.

Third, if you go to a gym, build some knee-strengthening exercises – leg extensions and squats – into your work-out. Speak to your gym about this as it's important to build balanced muscle groups that work together, so as not to pull the limb out of alignment. Some osteopaths also recommend glucosamine sulphate supplements (available in chemists and health food shops). This promotes cartilage repair and makes joints more resilient.

Blister advice

The old wives' tale says to rub surgical spirits or perfume into your feet to harden up the skin. This works, but large blisters can form between the hard layer and the soft skin beneath. So what can you do to prevent them? Try these if you're prone to blisters, or wearing in a new pair of boots.

■ Wear a thin sports-type sock under your thicker walking socks to lessen friction between the boot and your skin.

■ Rub talcum powder into your feet before you set off.

■ If you've got a 'hot spot' – an area that's prone to blisters no matter how far you walk – stick a hydrocolloid plaster (such as Compeed), or strap zinc oxide plaster, surgical tape or micropore tape over it before you set off.

Ordinary plasters fold and rub against the sock and your skin – especially in a moist environment – so they're more likely to give you a blister than save you from getting one!

■ Clothing

What you wear on the hill is largely a matter of personal choice. But in the last 20 years a revolution has swept through the outdoor world with the realization that new fabrics and designs can make walking far more comfortable and enjoyable, and even help save lives.

Base layers

Your body functions best when its core temperature is about 37°C (98.6°F). Fluctuations in ambient (air) temperature or increased muscle activity mean that you have to work harder to keep core temperature close to this critical value; indeed, just a couple of degrees either way, and you'll feel uncomfortably hot or distractingly cold. In extreme circumstances, a drop of just 4°C (39°F) in your core temperature can bring about loss of consciousness due to hypothermia, and a rise of 5°C (41°F) can cause the central nervous system to break down. It's therefore important to pay attention to the clothes you wear next to your skin, as these can either help or hinder your body's inbuilt thermostat.

The problem

At rest, the body pumps out about 0.06 litre (37cu in) of cooling moisture per hour, rising to 0.2 litre (12cu in) per hour during easy walks and light activity, and 1 litre (61cu in) per hour during heavy activity such as running. The evaporation of this liquid from the body's surface produces a very efficient cooling effect. However, during periods of intense activity, sweat can't evaporate quickly enough so it collects on the skin. The downside is that you wind up covered in sweat, which will carry on cooling you even if you stop and your body no longer needs to cool down.

The solution

To deal with increased perspiration, hikers need clothing that allows moisture to move away from the skin. Your base layer should also maintain a dry layer of air next to the skin to insulate against wind and cold. Here are the main factors you should consider when buying base layer clothing.

Wicking

To remove moisture that forms on the skin, you need to wear clothes that absorb sweat and move it through the fabric to the outside where it can evaporate. This process is called 'wicking', and it is the most important feature of a base layer.

In order for moisture to move through fabrics there has to be a driving force and this is related to the humidity and temperature difference between the inside and the outside of the fabric. So if the outside air gets warmer and wetter than the inside of the fabric, the wicking performance and breathability of the fabric are reduced. This is why hot and humid climates are the toughest conditions to contend with, while cold and dry climates are, in fact, the easiest.

Breathability

Breathable fabrics allow air to circulate, and water (in vapour form) to escape. This is an important factor in base layers, because water vapour trapped inside the clothing system will soon condense on your skin or on the inside of clothing. Some fabrics are, of course, more breathable than others.

Airflow

Increased airflow around the body helps shift water vapour away from skin. It also has a cooling effect, so you'll sweat less in the first place. This is why looser-fitting styles are ideal for hot climates.

Any fabric with a loose knit will be less wind-resistant, and so subsequent layers may have to be more windproof to compensate.

Coming clean

If sweat is trapped in the fabric, bacteria and unwelcome smells can multiply. Tests carried out by a leading clothing manufacturer, show that bacteria and trapped sweat can account for an increase of 20 per cent of a garment's weight. Stink-fighting chemical treatments are applied to base layers these days, though these will generally wash out over time. However, some specialist soap treatments such as Grangers Extreme Cleaner Plus will keep the worst smells at bay.

Some garments, such as those made with X-Static, contain silver to kill stench-causing bacteria. Merino wool evaporates moisture very effectively and so provides fewer opportunities for odour-causing bacteria to develop.

Base layers and layering

In some cases the clothes worn on top of a base layer will not allow moisture to pass through quickly enough. This means sweat will become trapped in the base layer, or next to the skin. So every garment in a layering system needs to be able to wick and breathe.

Base layer materials
Cotton

This natural fibre can soak up lots of water, but it doesn't wick it away. As the damp cotton clings to the skin it soon starts to feel cold and clammy, and will eventually draw heat from the body. This is why cotton is not recommended for base layers during high activity. However, it's soft, comfortable and highly breathable, so it's perfect for low intensity activity. It can be combined with other fibres to make useful knits such as polycotton and cotton nylons. These mixes are often quick drying, but have very little stretch. They're not suitable base layer fabrics, but are ideal for trousers and shirts.

Polyester

Polyester is hydrophobic (water-hating) and absorbs 60 times less moisture than cotton. The shape of each fibre enables it to wick moisture by capillary action from the inside of the garment to the outside. The majority of modern base layers are made from polyester, and one of the best known is DuPont Coolmax: this wicks more efficiently and dries five times faster than cotton.

Polypropylene

Polypropylene is hydrophobic and it too moves moisture across the fabric by capillary action. It is very durable and absorbs 40 times less moisture than polyester. Polypropylene is also 40 times more efficient than polyester at transporting moisture away from the skin. The down side is that it can get somewhat whiffy; however, the latest form of Helly Hansen Lifa offers less space for odour-generating bacteria

to grow, and so the days of 'Smelly Helly' are thankfully gone at last!

Merino wool

This is a highly breathable wool that can absorb around ten times more moisture than a synthetic yarn. Most importantly, it can wick moisture 27 per cent faster than synthetic fibres. New Zealand merino is used in Smartwool socks, while Australian merino is combined with other fibres to make Sportwool.

Silk

On its own, silk is a good insulator and has a luxurious feel. However, it's highly absorbent and doesn't wick well. It is easily degraded by UV exposure and perspiration. However, when it is used with other fibres, it adds strength, durability and softness.

The mid layer

A wicking base layer is little use under a cotton overshirt: your middle layers also need to be made from a fabric that keeps the sweat moving outwards, away from the body.

Polyester fleece, available in a variety of thicknesses and colours, is the most common fabric. The thicker the fabric the warmer it will be, although wearing a couple of thinner fleeces allows greater control over body temperature (because you can always take one off). Again, some fleeces are better than others in terms of softness, performance, warmth and durability – Polartec is the leading brand.

A basic fleece with two hip pockets and a front zip will work fine. But for regular hillwalking, look for one that's hooded in a longer cut (fleeces inevitably ride up) with a map-sized chest pocket that can be accessed while wearing a rucksack hipbelt.

The waterproof

After moving all that sweat away from your skin and out through your layers, it can now move out through the waterproof jacket – provided it's made from a breathable fabric. Just about every waterproof jacket is breathable these days, but there's always a trade-off between how breathable the garment is and its waterproofness.

Gore-Tex and Triplepoint fabrics will give you a good balance of waterproofness and breathability; and although Páramo garments are more breathable, they're less waterproof (water can force its way through the fabric, say, when kneeling). Pertex is more breathable still, but again, water will work its way through in heavy rain.

When choosing between the different fabrics, consider:

1 How fast you walk.
2 Your metabolism – do you sweat a lot?
3 Whether you'll be walking in heavy rain or light summer showers.

For example, if you walk fast, run or cycle, but not in heavy rain, you could get a highly breathable, but less waterproof jacket for maximum comfort.

The right gear

Technical mid layers

For hillwalking you need a mid-layer jacket that's warm, comfortable and practical when worn under a waterproof. Get the right mid layer, combine it with a waterproof jacket and a base layer, and you have a system of clothing that's ideal for anything from a walk in the park to a snowy alpine peak. But get it wrong and you'll get lost (because your map won't be to hand), cold (because the garment is the wrong shape or simply not warm enough) or ripped off (because the price is wrong and the jacket's features are not practical for walkers).

Most mid layers are sold to casual outdoor users, and thus they are not always ideal for the hill-goer who needs more practical features like map-sized pockets and a long cut to protect the lower back. A hood is a worthwhile feature too for winter hillwalking. If you're thinking of using your new jacket as an outer layer, consider getting a soft shell jacket instead. These usually employ some sort of laminated fleece such as Windstopper, or combine a soft fleece insulating layer with a weatherproof shell such as Pertex. Although these jackets can be extremely versatile, they aren't meant as waterproofs, so it is quite likely that you will end up carrying a lightweight waterproof jacket too.

Insulation

Mid layers are designed to provide insulation, with fleece being the benchmark material as it is lightweight, wind resistant and fast drying. Although a thick, warm fleece may seem the logical choice, when walking up a hill it may in fact prove too hot, so the thickest and warmest is not always best. Synthetic insulation, similar to that used in sleeping bags, is becoming common. It has the benefit of being more compressible and when made into a garment it is also often windproof, water resistant and very lightweight. But it can be too warm when worn under a waterproof.

Collar

A high collar helps to keep the neck warm while trapping warm air inside the jacket and preventing draughts. A drawcord may be provided around the neck to allow some adjustment; but if it is not, look for a close fit, or wear a neckwarmer to plug the gap.

Main zip

A full-length zip is standard as it makes the garment easy to put on and ventilate. A baffle behind the zip will help prevent draughts. Shorter-length zips mean the jacket will have to be put on over the head and don't allow as much ventilation, but they do save a bit of weight.

Cuffs

Look for close-fitting cuffs that may be elasticated or adjustable with Velcro. In hot weather you may want to pull the sleeves up to your elbows, so check if this is possible.

Water resistance

So that you don't have to be putting on a waterproof every five minutes, many mid layers now boast water-resistant qualities. These can be useful in light showers, but you'll still need a waterproof in heavy rain. If the garment is highly water resistant it often tends to be less breathable, and may also be heavier and more bulky.

Drawcords

To keep draughts at bay, look for a drawcord or elastication at the hem. Some have drawcords or elastication at the waist too.

Hoods

Not many people choose a mid layer with a hood, but they are very useful as the hood is always ready to whip on at a moment's notice and they will also protect the neck better than a hat.

Pockets

For serious hillwalking, when a map and compass are needed throughout the day, you can't beat a mid layer with large, map-sized chest pockets. However, lower pockets around the hips are more comfortable for the hands. So you may want a mid layer with two sets of pockets. But remember that you'll be wearing a rucksack, so check you can still access these pockets with your 'sack on.

Style

For practical use on the hills when walking, backpacking and scrambling, a long body is ideal as it won't ride up to expose your lower back.

Jackets

Wherever you do your hillwalking, at some stage you are going to need the protection of a jacket. It will keep off the rain, keep out the wind, and if you choose a 'breathable' jacket carefully, should keep you dry from within as well. General jackets are the jack-of-all-trades – just the job for backpacking, hill, valley and mountain walks in all weathers. A multi-activity jacket is designed for walking, biking, running and climbing, so might help you save money.

Lightweight waterproofs can weigh less than 600g (1.3lb) and are designed for walking, backpacking, scrambling, climbing and mountaineering. But if you're going out in the snow, you'll need a jacket that can comfortably withstand the harsher elements.

For a general-purpose walking jacket that will serve you year round, you should look for mid to high levels of waterproofness, breathability and durability. Lighter jackets tend to be less durable than heavyweight jackets: bear this in mind if you want a jacket for regular scrambling. The most durable fabrics are used to protect against abrasion from frozen earth, rock and ice. They are often more waterproof yet still as breathable or even more breathable than lower-priced alternatives. They are, however, often stiffer and heavier. Super-light fabrics are often just as breathable and waterproof as their heavier predecessors, but they may not be as durable. Ripstop threads within the fabric will prevent tears from becoming too long.

Zips

Normal zips are not waterproof, and 'water-resistant' zips are just that – not waterproof, so to keep the water out you need a double stormflap over the top. Double stormflaps make zips tricky to operate, so a single stormflap may be fitted instead. You may find exposed water-resistant zips under the arms for venting. Double zips are standard on most waterproofs. They allow you to open the jacket from the bottom and the top. Chinguards are often provided to prevent 'zip scratch' and for extra comfort in the cold. In winter, Velcro gets blocked with snow and freezes, so if you're looking for a winter jacket, choose a design with press stud or snap fastenings. An 'interactive zip' inside the jacket lets you zip a compatible fleece into the inside of the jacket. This is fine for everyday use, but not so good on the hill when you need a flexible layering system that allows layers to be peeled off quickly to control body temperature.

Body

Put the jacket on, zip it up and make sure its shape fits yours. Bend down as if tying your boot laces to gauge how much the jacket would ride up at the back when scrambling. Make sure you can sit in the jacket without it restricting movement or riding up around your neck. The jacket hem should remain still and the cuffs should not ride up. Women's jackets should have narrower shoulders, comfortable shaping around the chest, a smaller and higher waist, and wider hips.

Cuffs

A close-fitting adjustable cuff is essential to accommodate your gloves or mitts in winter, and to provide ventilation control. The best adjustment comes from a Velcro strap with elastication for comfort.

Hood

Ideally the hood should move with your head and never restrict vision. If the peak is wired or stiffened you can shape it around your face; if not then it may flop into your eyes, particularly in the wind. If you plan using the jacket for climbing, check that you can wear a climbing helmet under the hood; volume adjusters will improve fit. Rollaway hoods are a good idea, particularly on multi-activity jackets, as they can be tucked away when you're wearing a helmet.

Pockets

Most lightweight jackets are so short the pockets are on the chest to allow easy access while wearing a rucksack. Heavier jackets will have pockets lower down the body. Deep pockets may extend below the rucksack waistbelt, making it difficult to retrieve small items. Mesh-lined pockets will allow water to pass through if the zips are not protected by stormflaps. On a winter jacket, the best place for a map is in a pocket behind the stormflap but outside the main zip.

Ventilation

Look for extra ventilation options in the jacket, even though it will be 'breathable'. An easy-to-use front zip is essential. Adjustable cuffs allow air flow up the sleeves when loosened. Underarm zips or 'pit zips' may be provided and these can extend from the elbow to the waist. They provide added ventilation without the need to remove the jacket. Velcro stormflaps may be fitted to keep the zips waterproof, but water-resistant zips without stormflaps are less bulky and easier to use. Mesh pockets allow core venting, but may also allow water in.

Sleeves

Adjust the cuffs to fit snugly around the wrists, then raise both arms over your head and watch for the cuffs and hem riding up. If you want a jacket for scrambling then it's best if there is no movement in the cuffs or hem. For walking this is less of an issue, but it's still really annoying when clambering over a stile if a jacket rides up all the time. Women's jackets will have shorter sleeves with narrower cuffs than unisex jackets, but the sleeves should suit the length of your arms.

Drawcords

Check if the ends of the drawcords dangle freely. Drawcords may appear at the hood, hem and waist and should be neatly tucked away. If they dangle they can snag on gates, rocks or climbing harnesses and karabiners. On the hood they can whip you in the face. Only fair-weather walkers can live with flying drawcords!

Legware

What you wear on your legs while you're out hillwalking is again often a matter of personal taste. Many walkers prefer the 'tracksuit bottoms' look pioneered by Ron Hill in the 1980s. These leggings come in all manner of modern technical fabrics and allow maximum flexibility as well as easily slipping under a pair of waterproofs. Thicker leggings are available for winter use, or you can combine your summer ones with a good base layer long john. But not everyone suits leggings and there is now a wide range of more conventional-looking trousers/pants to suit most uses on the hill from trekking in the Greater Ranges to scrambling in the Scottish Highlands or day walks in the Alps.

Keeping your upper torso warm and dry is only half the battle. You should also invest in an effective pair of overtrousers to protect your legs from the ravages of wind, rain, cold and snow.

Fit and shape

For improved fit, comfort and style, look for tailored legs and waist. Overtrousers should fit over your normal walking legware and should neither restrict movement nor flap in the breeze.

Ankle cuff

Look for an ankle cuff that sits over the ankle cuff of the boot without letting water dribble into your boots. Some waterproofs designed with runners and cyclists in mind have elasticated ankle cuffs, but when used for walking, these often ride up and wet feet may be the result. Mountain pants often have an internal cuff. Adjustable ankle cuffs are the best design as they allow the trousers to fit over a variety of footwear from big winter boots to lightweight summer boots. Snap adjustment and drawcord adjustment works best, while Velcro adjustment has become popular (though it may clog when used in mud). Zipped bellows ankle cuffs work well too as they allow you to control a longer area of the trouser leg.

Materials

Fast-drying, wicking, non-creasing, lightweight and comfy fabric is best when you're travelling. Polycotton used to be the material of choice, but today it's been superseded by carefully woven nylon, which is superior. In waterproofs, look for breathable fabrics. This means your legs should stay dry while condensation and sweat are transported away. In general you'll get a more breathable, more waterproof and more durable fabric if you pay a higher price (for a similar design of overtrouser). However, some lightweight fabrics may be less durable than cheaper but heavier fabrics.

Fly

Not all trousers designed for the hill have a fly opening. Some trousers have a two-way zip which is ideal (if you're a man) for peeing when wearing a climbing harness or rucksack with a big hipbelt. Some trousers have no fly, though, and this is not ideal in winter or in really wet weather.

Pockets

You're bound to need pockets for valuables, especially if you're only wearing a T-shirt. A map-sized pocket for backpacking is ideal, but make sure you can access it while wearing a rucksack. For maximum security look for pockets with zipped rather than Velcro closures.

Stitching

For durability look for double or even triple stitching on important seams and bar-tacked seams at stress points.

Waist

A stretch waistband is a good start, while a belt or the ability to fit one is essential for longer trips away when you can lose a lot of weight. Braces (often called suspenders) are a really useful addition for mountaineering and scrambling.

Zip-off legs

These are a useful feature in many lightweight trekking pants. Once you've removed your zip-off legs, you don't want an ugly zip to show or to scratch your skin, so look for soft baffles over the top and behind the zips and make sure that the ends of the zip are neatly finished.

Waterproofness and breathability

A water-resistant coating such as Teflon is often applied to trekking pant fabric to fend off light splashes. This still allows the fabric to breathe but wicking performance is reduced, so those fabrics without a water-resistant coating are better for sweaty hiking!. Such coatings tend to wash out over time, but the protection can be restored using products from the Grangers or Nikwax range.

Freedom of movement

A diamond gusset under the crotch will ensure you can comfortably sit cross-legged in an airport for hours, which can be useful! But also look for careful placement of seams down the inside leg and around the waist, as these are areas that can readily chafe and become uncomfortable.

Side zips

These allow you to put waterproofs on without taking your boots off. Short zips are common on lower-priced trousers, while full-length side zips make it easy to put on waterproofs even while wearing crampons on your boots.

Boots

Your footwear is probably the most important piece of kit you will buy before you head for the hills. As with all hillwalking equipment, there is a huge range available to suit most budgets and the various terrains and conditions you're going to be out in. Choose the right boots for the right walk and you will find that you can spend more time on your navigating and admiring the views than worrying about blisters, sore feet and slippy soles.

Fit

No boot is worth having if it does not fit properly. The inside of a boot should be around 13–15mm (½–⅔ inch) longer than the length of your foot.

Support

A good shop will have an uneven test bed of wood or rocks for you to walk on. Do this and see if you can feel the terrain through your boots – if you can, you are looking at sore feet at the end of the day.

Waterproofness

Broadly speaking, lots of stitching on a boot means lots of holes for water to get in through, even though the best and most expensive three-season footwear comes with waterproof linings like Gore-Tex. Whether you want or need a lining on leather boots is a personal choice: with one, you get drier feet for the lifetime of the lining (but it often won't last as long as the boot and can sometimes fail within the year – worth remembering if you're tempted by fabric uppers), but also hotter and more humid walking. Some leather boots have cheaper unlined cousins that, if well and regularly waxed, are usually fine for all but the most prolonged boggy conditions. They also tend to be less sweaty and thus more comfortable in summer. All leather boots need regular treatment with wax (covering the stitching) to ensure a reasonable level of water-resistance.

Upper

Thickness of the uppers determines how much protection your foot can expect on rough terrain. To test it, squeeze the sides of the boot from above, comparing several models to get a feel for different thicknesses. The more sturdy the upper, the better the protection; and thick uppers also help keep the boot well shaped for longer and offer more support to your foot. The down side is that they weigh and cost more. Conversely, thin uppers (where you can squeeze the sides in easily) might be better if you plan on mostly keeping to valley paths. Although leather is still the most popular material, some boots use lightweight synthetic alternatives and winter boots may have extra insulation.

Ankle cuff

Ensure the ankle cuff is comfortable enough to walk in, particularly at the back of the heel where rubbing can be a problem. It should also rise high enough up the ankle to protect the foot against knocks and grazes from stray boulders and to prevent water getting in when stepping in puddles.

Footbed

Pull out the footbed and compare it to other boots: you will find they offer different levels of cushioning. Air vents help minimize sweat and some of the better versions will be contoured to offer improved support, particularly under the arch. Make sure the footbed fits the boot well, as creases and wrinkles mean blistering walks of entirely the wrong kind.

Tongue

A padded tongue is vital for a comfortable boot. Also look for a 'bellows' design that bridges the gap between tongue and upper to stop water or snow creeping in.

Midsole

The midsole is the hidden part of the boot between the outsole and footbed that determines a boot's stiffness. To assess it, grab the toe and heel and bend them together. Next, twist the toe while holding the heel. You should now have a good idea of how stiff the boot is – stiff is best for mountains and rocky ground, giving lots of support to stop feet tiring on a long day, whereas soft is better kept to woodland and valley paths. Four-season boots should be very stiff so that crampons stay fitted to the boot, and to enable the wearer to kick steps in hard snow.

Rubber rand

Look for a rubber rand between the sole and upper for greater durability. For rocky ground, one that runs right around the boot is perfect.

Toe box

To see how much protection you can expect from the toe box, press it with your thumb from the top, end and sides. Mentally replace your thumbs with rocks and you'll gauge how battered your feet will get on rough ground, scree or when scrambling. The stronger the toe box, the better the boots will perform on tough terrain, so if you are looking for a four-season boot, make sure there is plenty of internal stiffening around the toe.

Outsole

The all-important traction bit. Deep lugs on the outsole give better grip and a longer walking life. Compare the thickness of a pencil to the depth of the grooves on the sole – you want them to be deeper than the pencil for a useful level of traction and longevity (two pencils-deep is better). To prevent clogging, the lugs should be the thickness of two pencils apart. To keep you moving over snow, rocks or mud, modern rubber compounds have been developed that stick reasonably well in the wet without wearing out too quickly. Shallow treads wear down quickly especially when worn on rocky ground. Deep treads should cut through the snow and mud without problems, but some clog easily.

Cushioning

Find a hard surface and thump your heel down to get an idea of how much cushioning the boot offers. Cushioning is often made of EVA (ethyl vinyl acetate) or PU (polyurethane), or a mix of soft rubbers. It often varies across the sole unit, so be sure to stamp your whole foot on the hard surface, too. More cushioning is best for hillwalking and winter work; less will give you better sensitivity for scrambling and climbing. The best boots manage a good balance between the two.

Rucksacks/backpacks

For most general hillwalking, a 30–40 litre (1,831–2,441 cu in) rucksack is your trusty companion. Choose the right one and it should see you through even the most active periods of your hill career. If you're backpacking, your rucksack has to be big enough to carry everything you need and tough enough to survive the trip. Most rucksacks in the 60–75 litre (3,661–4,567 cu in) range can have their carrying capacity compressed or expanded to cater for trips when you might have to carry a greater or lesser amount of gear, so these really are multi-purpose load carriers. In between these two, the 40–50 litre (2,441–3,051 cu in) sacks will carry enough for a short lightweight camping expedition, or the extra gear you'll need in winter.

Durability

Even at the bottom end of the price range, rucksacks vary enormously in build quality and durability. The most durable rucksacks have double stitching, double layers of fabric and reinforced areas, but look at a few different models and you will soon be able to tell a well-built 'sack from a mediocre one. In general nylon is more durable than polyester, while Cordura is a popular and particularly durable form of nylon. Some buckles are made of very flexible plastic that allows them to bend without snapping, while lower-priced products may use buckles that easily snap when twisted or struck by rocks.

Attachments

At the very least, you need an ice axe attachment at the back; but side wand pockets – coupled with quick-release compression straps – are also good for axes, walking and tent poles.

Raincover

Few rucksacks offer any guarantees over waterproofness, but more and more are now being designed with a raincover built in. Remember that you will still need a waterproof liner to protect against persistent rain, and that raincovers are not usually very durable.

Stability

If you're negotiating rough ground or scrambling, you don't want your rucksack to leap around and knock you off balance. Chest straps hold the shoulder straps in place and keep the 'sack stable; these are virtually essential when carrying heavy loads.

Pockets

The number of pockets you need comes down to personal preference. If you use a hydration system, look for a pocket inside and an exit point for the hose. Side bellows pockets are useful as they leave the 'sack with a cleaner profile when empty, which is good for scrambling.

Lid

The top of the 'sack is covered by a lid. On 60 litre sacks or bigger, this may be designed to 'float' upwards, so that extra equipment can be carried. But in heavy rain, when the 'sack is only partially filled, this type of lid may allow water into the main compartment. Look for an extending lid that has a baffle between the back of the lid and the body of the rucksack to keep water at bay. To fend off rain that might creep in under the lid, better rucksacks have a deep weatherlock closure or snowhood with a drawcord.

Back length

Some sacks have adjustable back lengths, others come in different back lengths, and some are 'one size fits all'. To check if the size is right for you, tighten the waist- or hipbelt, adjust the shoulder straps and clip the chest strap together. The weight should bear down on your shoulders and hips. If the weight presses on the front of your shoulders, the back length may be too long. If the padding on the shoulder straps is more around the back of your shoulders, the back length may be too short.

Ventilation

Gone are the days of single foam-padded back systems that left you sweaty and hot and uncomfortable: most modern 'sacks incorporate plenty of ventilation in a variety of designs.

Compression straps

When your rucksack is half empty it can flap around, so look for compression straps on the sides. Best of all are straps with quick-release buckles.

Waistbelt or hipbelt?

If you plan on putting anything more than a waterproof and sandwiches in your 'sack, choose one with a decent hipbelt to transfer the weight to your hips. If you only plan on carrying small, light loads then you could be fine with a thinner waistbelt which, as the name suggests, goes around your waist. These are primarily designed for stability rather than the transfer of weight.

Freedom of movement

While great freedom of movement isn't critical for most everyday walking, if you plan on taking your 'sack scrambling at any point, it's important you won't be impeded by it.

Compartments

Many bigger rucksacks come with a main compartment and a lower compartment, with a removable divider between the two. This allows you to pack wet or dirty items, such as waterproofs or stoves, in the lower compartment, while the top compartment is reserved for dry and clean items.

What you wear on the hill is largely a matter of personal choice. But in the last 20 years a revolution has swept through the outdoor world with the realization that new fabrics and designs can make walking far more comfortable and enjoyable, and even help save lives.

Base layers

Closure position

Gaiters that close up the front are easy to fit and remove, while gaiters with a rear closure can be particularly annoying to fit.

Closure method

Most gaiters use a zip closure with a stormflap over the top to keep rain out, and this is held in place with Velcro and press studs. Some designs only have a Velcro closure which works OK, but it can be tricky to get a neat seal if the ends of the Velcro panels are not aligned properly. Press studs at the top and bottom make alignment of Velcro openings easier, but not all gaiters feature them.

Lace hook

The lace hook fits over the laces to hold the bottom of the gaiter in place. Try this with gloves on and think how hard it would be when your hands are cold and wet.

Fit

Gaiters come in different sizes and not all will fit your style of boot. With the gaiters on over your normal walking boots, check for a tight fit. If you can easily get your fingers under the gaiter and around the top of the boot, think how quickly mud and snow will get in too.

Top drawcord

Most gaiters have a drawcord at the top to seal the gaiter. Better designs place the drawcord locking toggle behind the knee but if it's placed at the front of the knee, it can make kneeling down painful.

Anti-snag

If your gaiters rub around the ankles, think how easily a crampon point could catch on them. The underfoot strap may also stick out on the inside of the boot, so make sure it is not going to snag.

Durability

Gaiters take a hammering from rock and crampons, so for hard use on rocky ground, or winter use with crampons, look for a durable design. That means reinforcement around the ankles, neoprene underfoot straps and a generally robust feel about the gaiter. Walkers heading for grass and mud can get by with less durable designs.

Underfoot strap

The strap that extends underneath the boot needs to be adjustable. This strap must be replaceable as it will wear out in the long run. Some are stitched in and not as easy to replace as straps that are held in place with buckles. Neoprene is the most durable material nowadays; webbing is less hard-wearing.

Breathability

All gaiters are a little sweaty, but some fabrics are less sweaty than others. Price is a good indicator – higher-priced gaiters of similar design are often made from more breathable fabric and these will be less sweaty.

Waterproofing

No gaiters are waterproof as the seams are not taped, so they will leak and water can easily creep in under the gaiter or through the zips – but some designs are more water-resistant than others. Look for a close fit around your boots and a stormflap over the front zip to help keep water out.

MOUNTAIN HARD WEAR

38

Headlamps

Since the 1980s the headlamp (or headtorch) has become a must-have piece of kit in most hillwalkers' rucksacks. Their robust and practical design, coupled with their ease of use, makes them invaluable for night time in the hills, whether by design or by unforeseen event. But recent developments have led to a profusion of different features. Choose a lamp which fits your needs best. Night vision can be lost immediately if you look at a light source, and it takes up to an hour for your eyes to re-acclimatize to the dark. So use your headlamp sparingly, and keep one eye closed whenever you use the lamp to look at the map, to save your night vision. LED lamps are easier on the eye and affect night vision far less than standard torches.

Tilting head

So that you can point the beam at the ground just ahead of you, the headlamp must have a tilting head. Ratchets are often used to control the tilt, while easy-to-adjust hinge bolts that allow tightening on the hill are also acceptable.

Bulb

Check the type(s) of bulb fitted. Tungsten bulbs are not very bright and don't have an exceptionally long burn time. Halogen bulbs offer the brightest output, but they'll use up your batteries the fastest. Krypton and xenon bulbs are a good compromise between the two. LED (light-emitting diode) bulbs are the current flavour of the month as they don't blow, so they don't need replacing; plus they offer daylight-balanced light with around 20 times longer burn times from batteries. As LED bulbs are not as bright as other bulbs, more than one is required for a bright light. Headlamps with a high power halogen bulb plus a set of three, five or seven LEDs are an ideal combination as you can save power by using the LEDs for general use, then switch to halogen when you need extra brightness or to project a beam.

Operation

How easy is it to operate the headlamp, and can you do it with gloves on? Put on a pair of gloves and switch between different power levels, and compare performances of different models. Lamps that switch between bulbs by rotating the front head or by using a rotating switch are generally the easiest method. Sliding switches are fairly simple to operate, but small press buttons are generally the most difficult to use with gloves.

Burn time

LEDs and other lights tend to dim over time as the batteries lose power, so judging burn time isn't easy. Black Diamond describes the burn time in terms of usable light which allows you to find an item at the bottom of your pack and see where you're putting your feet at night.

Batteries

Standard batteries are alkaline, but lithium batteries last almost twice as long and aren't affected by cold, though they are more expensive. Rechargeable batteries are the best choice for frequent users, but they don't last long between charges. However they are cheaper in the long run, and more environmentally friendly.

Fit and comfort

Put the headtorch on without a hat and consider the level of comfort. Can the straps be adjusted to fit your head shape? Any slight niggle now equals hours of discomfort on the hill.

What to eat

How to stay energized and hydrated throughout a long day on the hill is down to more than personal taste. With a little thought you can ensure your body is firing up ready for the strains you are about to put on it.

Especially if you're camping, it's tempting to start the day with just a cup of tea and a cereal bar, but overnight, your body will have used up much of its glycogen store (that's your primary energy source) so, unless you replenish it properly, you'll run out of energy by mid-morning.

Eat a balanced breakfast of whole cereal, juice, toast and perhaps even bacon and eggs if they're not too fatty. This will supply a healthy dose of carbohydrates, which your body breaks down into glucose and stores in your muscles as glycogen, providing a readily accessible source of energy. It also provides fibre, which delays the uptake of sugar into the blood so you'll get a sustained energy boost rather than an instant surge. Protein sources such as nuts and eggs will supply amino acids to rebuild and repair your body during periods of hard exercise.

If you're packing lunch, make up sandwich rolls with wholemeal bread. Mashed banana and honey is an excellent filling. Take a couple of extra pieces of fruit too and make sure you have something palatable to drink. A lunch like this will deliver a second super-hit of carbohydrates to provide further sustained energy. The fibre in the wholemeal rolls will help to control the sugar-rush from the chocolate you're likely to snack on later, too. In addition to carbohydrates, the fruit contains valuable liquid: so this'll help keep you hydrated (an

orange is 86 per cent water and surprisingly even the humble banana scores an impressive 71 per cent).

For a longer-term hill-food plan, base your diet on these staples, then add a little of whatever else you fancy. All will survive a few days in your pack and offer a good energy source (measured in kcal-to-weight ratio) – although a few earn their place for their taste (measured in ahh-factor-to-weight ratio) too.

Don't underestimate how much energy you'll need: walking uphill uses 2½ times the calories of walking over level ground.

Where you get that energy from is important too. Aim to get the bulk from carbohydrates: your on-the-hill diet should consist of 60 per cent carbs, 20 per cent protein and 20 per cent fat. This high percentage of carbs will keep your body fuelled with readily available energy – and by choosing starchy (as opposed to sugary) carbohydrates, you'll get a steady stream of energy, rather than an instant high followed by a draining low.

Fat provides energy too, but it takes far longer to digest, and actually slows the absorption of the carbs, so keep high-fat foods for the end of the day, rather than while you're walking. And the protein is essential for muscle repair, to ensure you're fit for the following day.

Quick-cook pasta is the easiest on-the-hill dinner to prepare: choose wholemeal for a 284kcal serving (56g/2oz carbs). Stir in pesto, cheese spread (it's the business!) or tomato purée, plus a handful of dried onions and slices of salami.

Dried sliced onions may not be the most glamorous hill food, but their taste-to-weight ratio is unbeatable. Chuck a handful into your pot of boiling pasta for an instant meal upgrade.

Tomato purée in a tube is a low-fat, high-carb, easily transportable pasta topping. Squeeze it onto a roll or a strip of beef jerky too – it tastes far better than you'd imagine.

Salami sticks such as Peperami earn their place in your pack on account of taste – plus a decent 22 per cent protein content.

Wholemeal pitta bread is a packable, stackable 'sack staple. Each pocket gives 146kcal with a substantial 26g (0.9oz) of complex carbs. Fill with cheese spread or peanut butter.

Rice cakes aren't as dull as they sound: try the sesame garlic flavour for a crunch that tastes of mild Twiglet or pretzel. They'll propel you up hill after hill, with over 80 per cent carbohydrates providing a seriously sustained energy boost.

Fruit leather – one 14g (0.5oz) strip gives 10g (0.3oz) carbs and no fat.

A tube of **cheese spread** should be packed in your 'sack purely for taste purposes. While the cheesy spread is a valuable protein source, be aware of its 20 per cent fat content and spread it on thinly.

Oatcakes provide sustained energy, so they make a good lunch. One oaty round delivers a punching 46kcal, of which over 60 per cent comes from carbohydrates. Check the nutritional info and choose a brand with no added sugar though. Scrape on the cheese spread thinly!

Muesli is the hill breakfast of choice. With a whopping 32g (1.1oz) of carbohydrates per 50g (1.75oz) serving, it'll get your day off to an energetic start. Mix with milk powder before packing, then add water at camp. Look for no added sugar and a fat content less than 10 per cent. Try topping with hot water instead of cold or, for extra energy, orange juice.

Wholemeal bread rolls are your staple carb-rich holder of tasty fillings. Try with fruit spread, honey and banana, or peanut butter.

Beef jerky is the perfect foodstuff for repairing your battered body overnight. With 44g (1.5oz) protein per 100g (3.5oz), it'll provide the necessary building blocks to ensure you're in good shape for the following day.

Peanut butter is here for its protein content – 2.3g (0.08oz) per teaspoonful (a valuable source if you're a vegetarian). It's also very high in fat, which is a rich – but slow to digest – energy source. Dig into a plastic jar of the nutty gunk in the evening, so you've time to digest it overnight, for maximum benefit .

Dates pack the highest energy boost of all fruits: each date delivers 46kcal, of which 75 per cent comes from carbohydrates. Make sure the dates you buy aren't coated in glycerine, though.

Raisins offer an instant pick-me-up. While your overall aim is to provide your body with sustained energy, sometimes you need a surge of energy to reach a summit. Raisins also provide potassium, which your body needs to convert sugar in the blood into energy.

Fig rolls (fig Newtons) make a fine snack stuffed with carbohydrates: each biscuit provides a carb-rich 70kcal and a sweet, feel-good fix.

Unsweetened fruit spread is a rucksack must-pack if you have a sweet tooth. Although it's full of sugar, it's released fairly slowly, so won't give you the instant high, followed by the plummeting low, that the sugar in a chocolate bar would.

Jaffa Cakes are the answer if you can't survive a few days without chocolate. While an average chocolate biscuit contains 4g (0.14oz) of hard-to-digest fat, a Jaffa Cake only has 1g (0.03oz) fat, and is 80 per cent carbohydrate.

Dried fruit gives you all the sustained energy benefits of fruit without carrying the weight of 80 per cent water content. Buy ready-dried fruit or make your own: slice the fruit (apples work well) thinly and put in a single layer on a baking tray. Place in the oven at the lowest temperature setting (around 60°C/140°F). It'll take up to four hours, but check them every 20 minutes: opening the oven door frequently will also help remove moist air and improve the result. Keep in zip-lock bags.

Malt loaf is the ultimate energy-dense food: the entire loaf weighs a paltry 225g (7.9oz), but you'll get 697kcal for your money, of which 146g (5.1oz) is carbohydrates and only 5g (0.18oz) fat. And somehow it manages to taste just as good after being squashed in your 'sack for days.

Cereal bars are transportable tanks of energy. Even after a breakfast high in carbohydrates, you'll only have 60–90 minutes of hillwalking time before your body runs out of readily available energy – so you need to refuel every hour. Stock up on energy or cereal bars, but check the nutritional info first: many are horrendously high in fat, which will slow your digestion and actually impede the energy flow – don't touch any cereal bar that's over 20 per cent fat.

Seeds (take your pick from pumpkin or sunflower) provide a snack that's a good source of slowly released energy. They also pack a valuable protein punch – mix a variety at home and carry them in a zip-lock bag.

Orange juice should be viewed as a food. At the end of a long day, this carbohydrate-rich rocket fuel will revive your body almost instantly, taking just 15 minutes to be digested.

Horlicks – don't laugh now – is great hill food. Buy the Light Malt version that uses boiling water, rather than milk, and you have a hot drink that feeds you 23g (0.8oz) of carbohydrates.

Fruit teabags make a far better on-the-hill brew than regular tea or coffee, which both contain diuretic caffeine that'll dehydrate your body.

Bananas are the Superman of hill foods. Made up of 76 per cent water, 23 per cent carbohydrate and not a trace of fat, they're the ideal regular snack to keep your body going between meals. Add a sliced banana to your muesli or rice pudding, too.

Nuts – don't leave home without them. Packed with carbohydrates, protein and fat, they're a great energy source: the average Brazil nut packs a whopping 25kcal. But keep them for evening refuelling: the high fat content will slow digestion, so nuts won't deliver energy efficiently while you're walking. Nuts also provide magnesium, which helps to guard against muscle-burn from lactic acid production.

Rice pudding – yes, really. Once you've stopped walking, you have a two-hour window in which to replenish your muscle glycogen ready for the following day. After this window, the process is far less efficient. So before you erect the tent or brew a cuppa, sink a 200g (7oz) carton of rice pudding: it'll provide 35g (1.2oz) of energy-rich carbohydrate, 7g (0.24oz) of protein to aid muscle repair, and 3g (0.1oz) of fat (which your body will now have time to digest). Add raisins or a dollop of fruit spread.

Green pesto in a tube turns dull pasta into high-class cuisine. Keep it for the evening though, as its fat content is high.

Runny honey in a plastic squeezy bottle is an on-the-hill must. Just one tablespoon packs a cool 51kcal, with under 0.1g (0.003oz) fat.

Pocket fuel

Flagging on the hills? The fastest way to beat fatigue, boost your blood sugar levels and top up your muscle glycogen store is to eat carbohydrate – as soon as possible. But although you might think sugary foods will release their carbohydrate into your system faster than starchy ones, it's not quite that simple.

In fact, the glucose from some starchy foods is absorbed more quickly than others – for instance, the starch in white bread is digested more quickly than the starch in baked beans. Also, sugars that occur naturally in fresh and dried fruits are absorbed more slowly than the highly processed starches used as thickeners in many soups and pasta sauces.

Such differences in the speed of sugar absorption are measured and rated according to the glycaemic index (GI). Foods with a high GI (85–100) produce a rapid rise in blood glucose; foods with a low GI (less than 60) are far slower.

So, when you're tonking across the hills, it's best to eat foods with a high GI (see below) as your body can make good use of the energy. However, if you load up on high GI foods such as chocolate, cakes and biscuits when you're just sitting around, your blood sugar and insulin levels will rocket, then rapidly fall. This is known as the 'rebound effect' which can make you feel lethargic.

The glycaemic index should only be used as a guide since the values refer to single foods. In practice, we eat a mixture of foods. Other food components – fibre, fat and protein – interact with carbohydrate and tend to slow down its digestion and absorption.

Foods that make you go zoom (in order of saintliness)

1 Bananas (GI 90)
The GI of a banana varies according to how ripe it is: green ones contain a large amount of starch, which can be difficult to digest. The starch is converted into sugar as part of the ripening process which is why yellow/black fruits will taste sweet. This food comes in its own natural wrapping with a good dose of potassium, which is an important mineral for muscle metabolism.

2 Dried fruit (GI 31-64)
The GI varies considerably between dried apricots (31) and raisins (64). The sugar content of apricots is locked within a fibrous structure which your digestive system has to break down before the sugars are released. Nevertheless they can help build and maintain your blood sugar level (rather than produce a sudden surge). Like most orange-red fruits, apricots are packed with beta-carotene, a powerful antioxidant, but most brands also contain sulphur dioxide to preserve their colour.

3 Oatcakes (GI 55)
Easy to carry and a good source of slow-release carbohydrate and fibre. Sandwich them together with honey or jam for a brilliant combination of fast- and slow-release carbohydrate fuel.

4 Chocolate (GI 49)
It may be surprising to see this food relatively high on the list. However, there are times, as every chocoholic knows, when only chocolate will do! As well as the energy-boosting effect of sugar, the psychological lift when you're homeward bound should not be underestimated. If you enjoy chocolate, buy the sort with a high percentage (over 50%) of iron-providing cocoa solids rather than the sweetshop varieties which are simply cheap imitations made from poor-quality vegetable fat and sugar.

5 Orange juice (GI 75)

This is a lazy way of eating fruit, but it does provide a good dose of fast-release carbohydrate along with some vitamin C and potassium. As a juice the sugars are already in solution for ease of digestion, hence the high GI.

6 Flapjacks (GI 60)

These can be a wonderful mixture of oats, golden syrup, butter, dried fruits, nuts and seeds – if you make them yourself! Many mass-produced bars are stuck together with hydrogenated vegetable fat, which is something to avoid as it slows down the release of sugars and clogs your arteries.

7 Cheese and pickle wholemeal sandwich (GI 55)

The wholemeal bread and pickle provide fast-release carbohydrate but the fat in the cheese will slow down the digestion and absorption of the sandwich. The trick is to choose a strong mature cheddar but to use less of it; thus your sandwich will have plenty of flavour, but less fat.

8 Crisps/potato chips (GI 50)

These are high in fat, which tends to interfere with the digestion and absorption of the carbohydrate from the potato. Nevertheless, these are one of life's comfort foods. Make sure you drink enough water as well, since you're likely to be dehydrated at the end of the day.

9 Nutri-Grain cereal bar (GI 65)

This is something you should eat only in desperation. It's a synthetic mixture of highly refined carbohydrates stuck together with thickeners and emulsifiers. Sure this bar will give you a boost of sugars, but there are much better choices available.

10 Pork pie (GI 25)

Your average pork pie is so high in fat, there's lard oozing from every pore! The pastry and so-called meat is low in carbohydrate and what little there is has to struggle to be digested among the greasy gruel that slides around in your intestines after a mouthful. These are likely to drain your energy levels rather than boost them.

Now for a little bit of what you fancy!

Does your après-hill grub meet energy emission targets? You might be in for a pleasant surprise…

Cakes and cookies

These get a definite halo. The best time to eat cake is within the two-hour window after finishing a strenuous day on the hills. During this time, your muscle glycogen stores are low and screaming out for more carbohydrate to refill these fuel tanks. Fruit cake, malt loaf, gingerbread and Madeira cake are the best since they have more carbohydrate and less fat compared with your average buttercream-filled sponge.

Chips/French fries

An OK choice since the potatoes do provide some carbohydrate. The frying process adds fat to the mix which will slow down digestion and keep you feeling full for longer.

Baked potato and tuna

A great choice which provides a useful mixture of carbohydrate and protein. During a day in the hills your muscles suffer a certain amount of wear and tear. While you sleep, the damage to muscle fibres is repaired but this process requires protein. Tuna fish too provides a good dose of essential fats, which can also assist in the repair process.

Glass of beer

Fluid replacement is usually high on the list of priorities when you come off the hills. But... if you're severely dehydrated, beer is not the best option. The good news is that one glass of beer does have some healthy properties; the alcohol it contains has a positive effect on the levels of HDL particles (or 'good' cholesterol) in the blood, helping to reduce fatty deposits in the arteries. Regular aerobic exercise is good for HDL cholesterol too, so the combination of a day in the hills followed by a trip to the pub gets the healthy thumbs up!

Stay hydrated

So you know everything you need to know about hydration, right? Swig several gallons of water a day; coffee's a no-no; drink before you get thirsty, etc...

Well, the latest research shows it may be time to think again. Apparently it is possible to over-hydrate. It's called hyponatremia, also known as 'water intoxication'. If you drink too much during strenuous exercise, you flush much-needed sodium and other minerals out of your bloodstream. In extreme cases this can lead to seizures, fluid in the lungs and even death!

So I don't have to drink as much?

Experts now recommend you drink enough that your wee remains pale, clear and copious – but not so copious that you're loo-bound every half hour. Nutritionists admit that they're not sure if we need to drink eight to ten glasses of water a day, and say that simply drinking when you get thirsty could be sufficient.

What about sports drinks?

Sports drinks containing up to 6 per cent carbohydrates (sugars) will be absorbed into the body just as rapidly as water and are therefore beneficial for their extra energy and sodium. However, sports drinks containing more than 10 per cent will have negative effects.

Can I still have a morning coffee?

Yes, you can! Caffeine's not as dehydrating as once thought. In fact, a mug in the morning can count as one of your cups of water for the day. It will have you running to the toilet more often than water, but you'll only lose half of what went in.

So were they wrong about booze, too?

Unfortunately not. Alcohol still isn't doing you any favours in the fluid replacement department. A pint of beer not only won't count towards your daily intake, but experts suggest you need to consume a full glass of water for every pint you drink.

Drink more at altitude

The atmosphere up high is cold and incredibly dry. When you inhale, the air's warmed and humidified, sucking heat and moisture from your body. The higher you go, the faster you breathe, so the more you lose. Increased exhalation means you lose more carbon dioxide than usual, leaving your blood too alkaline. To right this the kidneys excrete alkaline bicarbonate into the urine. You must drink to help this flushing process.

Route planning

Before you head into the hills for a day's walking, there are a few things you can do to make your time there more enjoyable and safer.

Why are you going?

Perhaps the most important of these is to plan where it is you are going, and before you do that, you should make yourself aware of a few important details. It may sound like navel gazing, but first ask yourself what your aims are for the day. Do you want to climb a specific hill? Do you want a day 'in the mountains' without necessarily being at the highest point? Do you want good views, or an interesting scramble? Do you mind if it gets foggy or it rains? If you are going in a group – family or a bunch of mates – do they share the same aims for the day?

Think through these motivational aspects and you will probably ensure that everyone goes out properly equipped and prepared for the walk ahead.

Plan ahead

When you're planning the walk itself you can adopt one of two approaches. For a formally organized group walk, maybe with a club, a youth group or a school party, it's a good idea to have a fairly rigid structure to the walk. Not only does this mean everyone can be briefed on what to expect, but also you can do some nifty prior planning, if you are leading the group. Filling in a route card (see page 47) will prompt you to think about your escape routes, the experience of your group and the equipment you are carrying. Carefully studying the map beforehand should alert you to the potential dangers – where are the cliffs to avoid? Which slopes can be descended quickly? What are the orientation points on the skyline?

You can also make more detailed routefinding notes. How many paces to the top of the descent path from the summit? What direction is it in? You can even make a note of the critical bearings, which will save you having to sit down with a map and figure them out from first principals when you get there. Since many hillwalkers have their greatest navigational difficulty negotiating the fields, fences and walls which tend to come between them and the open country, it's a good idea to study these too, and scribble yourself a few aide memoires if necessary. That way you can begin your walk as cool veterans with local knowledge, and not feel like the prat in the hat with the big map.

Hang loose

But for a good day in the hills you don't necessarily have to decide every turn in advance. Sometimes it is more satisfying, and safer, to make informed decisions on the hoof. In bad weather, or when winter conditions prevail, you will need the flexibility to make route changes. Your planning therefore has to take into consideration how much daylight you have, how much food you are carrying, what the weather will be like (remember many adverse conditions like high wind or snow will slow you down significantly), and what the terrain will be like. If you're taking a flexible approach, you'll still need to let others know your general aims. A simple route card can cover the basics about the area you are walking in and how many people are in the group and what their equipment and experience is like. Don't forget to finish the job though. Make sure you confirm you have completed the day safely with whoever you told your plan to, even if you never made it past the pretty pub in the valley bottom!

Guidebooks and getting there

If you're exploring a new area, a guidebook is a handy reference tool, but make sure you back it up with a good map. The outdoors is a changing world and it may be some years since the guidebook writer strolled your particular bit of hill. Never rely on a guidebook alone for navigation – if you make one little error, you won't have any reference tools to get you back on track. Where guidebooks come into their own (and their peculiar cousins, the books of mountain lists) is for opening up new areas of hill country for you – getting you away from the tourist routes up the big name hills on to the back-country classics that only the hillwalkers know. Read the dramatic and appealing entries, gape at the pictures taken on Hasselblads at dawn, then leave them at home on the coffee table and plan your own informed explorations with a map, compass and GPS.

If you're not constrained by having to start and finish at your car, a linear route can make for a very satisfying

day out. Local transport maps and timetables are usually available on the web. Check them beforehand, and if possible see if you can contrive a route that allows you to walk back to your car, rather than aiming to catch the last bus or train. In upland areas, public transport is often a seasonal phenomenon, so double check that the service you're relying on will actually be running when you need it. The same is true of cable cars and chairlifts – and these are also often weather dependent. If you are planning to finish your walk at the top of a cable car route, it is prudent to aim to arrive there with enough time and energy to walk down to the valley in daylight.

Overnighting needs more detailed planning, so you'll find more information on this in pages 96-107.

pages 96-107.

Pre-fill route cards

Before heading for the hills, it's a sensible precaution to fill out a route card to leave at your B&B/hostel. But how often have you scribbled down the essential details during breakfast, worrying it's time you were on your way?

We all have a store of must-do-soon routes in our head – so fill in the route cards for them now. It's surprising how long this takes to do well: you'll need to scrutinize the map and work out potential escape routes as well as bearings between main features. Use the route card below as a template, and note your intended plans. Then all you need do on the day is fill in the missing info such as party size, equipment, date and times.

Route card	Walkers in party	Staying at	Mobile number Vehicle details / reg
Date			
Start point	Grid ref	Start time	
Waypoints	Grid ref	Bearing	
Finish point	Grid ref	Est. finish time	
Potential escape route		Equipment taken	

Estimating route times

Since William Wilson Naismith calculated his universal rule back in 1892, route-planning has been much easier. He reckoned that most folk walk at 5km per hour (3mph), taking an extra half-hour for every 300m (1,000ft) of ascent. In practice it's easy to apply: measure your route in kilometres and then divide this number by five to get an approximate time in hours; then add an extra minute for each 10m contour line you climb; and, if the descent is continuously steep, add an extra minute for every three 10m contour lines you descend.

But there's just one problem: Naismith's rule gives a standard time to complete a route, whether you're a fit fell runner or an arthritic crone. Your task is to personalize Naismith's rule to your own fitness level using a set of figures known as Tranter's corrections. This is what you do:

Scour a map to find a slope that climbs 300m (984ft) in 800m (2,625ft). Conduct some time trials on your chosen slope to measure in minutes how long it takes you to walk up the slope at your normal pace (racing up will render your calculations useless).

The table below shows Tranter's corrections: it adjusts route times calculated according to Naismith's rule to give you a more realistic estimate (in hours) in line with your fitness level. For example, if using Naismith's rule you worked out a route would take you 6 hours, and you scaled your test slope in 25 minutes, your realistic route time is 7 hours.

Use the table to customize your times further: if you're carrying a heavy pack, the weather's awful or you know you're going to be crossing difficult ground, drop one fitness level for each factor counting against you.

Time a route would take you according to Naismith's rule (hours)

Fitness level: time you took to climb 300m in 800m (minutes)

	2	3	4	5	6	7	8	9	10	12	14	16	18	20	22	24
15	1	1½	2	2¾	3½	4½	5½	6¾	7¾	10	12½	14½	17	19½	22	24
20	1¼	2¼	3¼	4½	5½	6½	7¾	8¾	10	12½	15	17½	20	23		
25	1½	3	4¼	5½	7	8½	10	11½	13¼	15	17½					
30	2	3½	5	6¾	8½	10½	12½	14½								
40	2¾	4¼	5¾	7½	9½	11½			don't even attempt it!							
50	3¼	4¾	6½	8½												

Recognize dangerous terrain

If you venture from the path on an emergency descent, it's vital you don't choose a route that will lead you into further trouble. Contours on British Ordnance Survey Landranger (1:50,000) maps are shown in intervals of 10m. On very steep terrain, some of these contour lines may not be shown because they're stacked so closely together. As a general rule of thumb, if there's one line missing between the thicker 50m contour lines, the terrain is just about possible to descend. If there are two missing between the 50m lines, it's not.

It's also handy to be able to guess-timate whether a stream will be just a jump across or a serious wade. On a Landranger map, streams and rivers are marked three ways:

- Single thin blue line: less than 4m (13ft) wide.
- Single thick blue line: 4–8m (13–26ft) wide.
- Two blue lines with a tint between: more than 8m (26ft) wide.

Global Positioning Systems

GPS receivers are now cheaper and more accurate than ever. On the hill you'll see no end of walkers staring blankly at their little screens. But is it vital kit? It depends on how you use it.

GPS stands for 'Global Positioning System', a system of 27 Earth-orbiting satellites developed by the USA. Data from them can be used to pinpoint any location on the globe using a GPS receiver. GPS receivers use different numbers of channels to track the satellites. A 12-channel parallel receiver is now the most common. This is better than a six- or eight-channel parallel receiver as it has more 'eyes on the sky' which allows it to find the satellites more easily, particularly in built-up areas or in woods. The better the receiver, the more chance there is that the unit will be able to make an accurate fix on your position.

Map datums

Map datums describe the irregular shape of the Earth for a particular region. Different maps have different map datums because the Earth is shaped differently in different regions. So GPS users must reference their GPS receivers to their maps. In the UK the GPS receiver must be set to OSGB or GRB36. For most European countries you need European 1950 set as the datum. Most GPS receivers are set to WGS84 (World Geodetic Survey 1984) in the factory but sadly none of the instruction manuals makes it clear that you have to change this. If you want to store maps on the GPS receiver you'll need lots of memory too. At least 24MB is good, but 56MB is even better.

Coordinate systems

A grid of horizontal and vertical lines is provided on maps of the UK so that you can pinpoint a location with a grid reference. But

the two most common coordinate systems in the world are LAT/LON and UTM. If you are using a GPS receiver in the UK, you must set the coordinate system to one that matches the coordinate system on the maps you are using, which is usually referred to as OSGB, ord srvy GB, or British Grid. The factory setting for most GPS receivers is LAT/LON. If you are travelling around the world then make sure the unit has the appropriate coordinate systems for the map you are using.

When to use a GPS

For the most part walkers and backpackers still need to read maps and use compass techniques when navigating; but a GPS receiver is a useful addition to their armoury, particularly when they find themselves in situations where conventional navigation is unreliable, such as crossing the Cairngorm plateau in a blizzard, or travelling through areas where the maps are poor, such as in many countries where recreational walking has not been a traditional priority. In forests a GPS can be very useful as it is difficult to navigate through these areas with a map at the best of times, although GPS receivers do need a clear 'view' of the sky to work. They can also provide a useful backup for when conventional map and compass techniques fail (see also page 73–74).

Satellite screen

This shows a 'sky view' of the satellites above you. The bars show signal strength and, below that, your location as a grid reference. GPS works on a 'line of sight' system, so the signal strength is blocked or weakened by cliffs, hills, anything metal, heavy tree cover or even someone standing next to you. If the unit has been moved to another part of the country while switched off, or it hasn't been used for a couple of months, it will take time to locate its position. This is normally less than a minute.

Map screen

There's a basic built-in map with around the same level of detail as a road map. When you have programmed in the points that you want to navigate between (waypoints), these appear on the screen. But the map screen doesn't show mountains, contour lines or obstacles.

Furthermore, when you plot a route, the GPS can't take into account the fact that there may be dangerous ground in between the waypoints, it will only show the most direct route. So always carry a map and compass and know how to use them.

Trip computer screen

This page has a variety of data fields to choose from, and you can customize it to show the data you want. Choose from moving speed, average speed or maximum speed; total ascent/descent; distance covered; distance to next waypoint or final destination; moving and stopped time; and estimated time of arrival. It will even show times of sunset and sunrise. Undoubtedly this page has very practical applications, but its greatest value is probably just the sheer interest factor as you go back through post-trip statistics.

Compass

The compass has to be calibrated at the start of every walk. This involves turning the unit through 360 degrees slowly (in one direction) for about a minute. Some GPS compasses don't function from a standing start. You need to start walking to get them working and then correct your bearing.

An electronic compass is subject to the same variations as a base-plate compass, so if you're in an area with strong magnetic fields (the Cuillin ridge on the Scottish island of Skye is the classic example), extra attention must be paid to the terrain to avoid error.

Altimeter

This uses an electronic pressure sensor to calculate altitude. This can be worked out from the air pressure and is usually accurate to within 3m (10ft). You also have the option to select an altitude based solely on satellite positions, which is accurate to 30m (98ft). Because air pressure changes over the day, there will be a cumulative inaccuracy which can be virtually eliminated by recalibrating at a known altitude – a spot height, for example. And if you want to keep it absolutely accurate, the most often that you'll have to re-calibrate is every couple of hours when the weather is bad.

Main menu

Program in favourites, waypoints and points of interest, such as the start of a scramble, a good place to cross a river that you want to be sure of finding on the way back, an ice-cream van or where you stashed your sandwiches... Cities will show up on your GPS screen, but it can't tell you anything about the place other than the fact that it exists. This screen displays time and date, backlight status and power levels.

Track log

This is an automatic function which downloads data at set points along your walk. It works by leaving a 'breadcrumb trail'; a snapshot of the date, time, location and altitude. Because of memory limitations, if you're going on a longer trip, say for a two-week trek in the Himalayas, you can set the GPS to 'drop a breadcrumb' less frequently. By spacing out these points you can accurately record up to ten active days.

When using the track log facility, it's important to remember that the signal can be weakened (making the data less accurate) if you put the unit inside your rucksack. To ensure that the GPS receives a strong signal, carry it in the top pocket of your rucksack, or in a chest pocket – upright and facing outward – so that the aerial is in the best possible position.

Setting up your GPS

After switching your GPS on, you must set it up for use. A GPS unit can be used anywhere in the world, but it has to be told which data to use before you go walking (see coordinate systems page 49). The position might then look something like this: SU 37733 BNG 20529
- SU is the two-letter reference for the 100km grid square
- 37733 is the easting, to 1m resolution
- BNG means British National Grid
- 20529 is the northing, to 1m resolution

For walking purposes, a six-figure grid reference is all you need, so to get this, knock off

the last two numbers on each line. This gives you a grid reference of 377205.

Make sure the statute (distance measurement), is set to metric or your local equivalent. This done, and with the altimeter and compass calibrated, you're ready to navigate!

Planning the route

Plotting your route on digital mapping programs is simple but, when using with GPS in mind, not entirely intuitive. Remember the GPS will navigate between waypoints, so rather than following every twist in the path on the map, just place them at critical turns so you follow the general direction of the paths, as shown by the blue lines on our route. Think of the GPS as you would a compass – it will point you in the right direction but it's still up to you to follow the track on the ground. The advantage is that, unlike a compass (which will point towards a bearing), the GPS direction arrow will always lead you directly to the next assigned waypoint.

Once you have your main route mapped out, change those waypoint numbers to meaningful text (on some maps you won't be able to name Nodes, so insert waypoints where you need more label detail).

Some software allows you to access aerial photography to check whether the paths on the ground match the paths on the maps – sometimes they don't, and this can affect how you input your waypoints.

Once you have all your potential routes mapped and have inserted any alarms (see

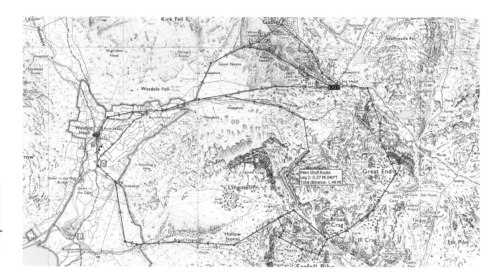

above), simply transfer the data to the GPS. Then print off route cards to help you interpret waypoints en route, print off the map, and everything is synchronized for the hill.

Escape routes

You can pre-program a GPS with escape routes or alternatives, allowing you to make different route choices on the hill (see diagram, right). Just mark the new route and give it a distinctive name to appear under 'Routes' when transferred to the GPS ('Split' or 'escape' as above). Then you can switch between options as you walk.

Losing signal

A GPS receiver needs to be in the line of sight of at least three satellites in order to work, and accuracy increases as it picks up more. As such there are places where you will lose signal. Understand the limitations of GPS in steep

gorges or areas of heavy woodland and return to map and compass: a GPS never replaces the need to carry them.

Alarms

Some GPS units feature alarms that sound when you get to within a pre-determined distance of a certain point (proximity alarms), or when you leave your intended route (off-course alarm). Set an alarm to warn you of upcoming forks in the path, or for when you come within a certain distance of a cliff edge.

Batteries

GPS units eat batteries at a fair old rate, so make sure you carry sufficient spares. When you are not using functions like the barometric altimeter, turn them off to help conserve the power. In cold conditions, consider using lithium batteries – lighter but more expensive than normal alkalines, their performance doesn't suffer in low temperatures. Colour screens eat batteries faster but look nicer.

Post-walk analysis

After your walk you can download the 'Track' – the trail of your actual walk stored on the GPS – on to your mapping software and see how accurately you followed your intended route. Ours is the wobbly red line on the map. It's fascinating to see how your movements on the ground correlate to the paths on the map or the aerial pictures. Plus you can overlay your speed to see which bits you did fastest, or even pull up an accurate elevation profile. Then finally, to show off in the pub, you can do an actual walk or fly-through for the route you actually followed.

Weather in the hills

The British are said to be always talking about it. The North Americans even have a TV channel dedicated to it. There isn't a corner of the globe that isn't covered by a satellite image or webcam and forecast. Which is great for those of us who want to head for the hills, because now, with a little extra knowledge, we will always be able to anticipate the weather conditions – which means wearing and-carrying the right kit and keeping clear of the dangerous stuff.

It helps to know a little bit about how weather works before you switch on the forecast. Unless you are getting a specialist hill conditions report (often these are seasonal, so the web is the best place to start), you'll need to interpret the mainstream forecast, which really only applies to the urban areas.

Some weather theory

Weather is how we experience climate. It's the day-to-day, look-out-of-the-window stuff that brings us rain, sun, snow, wind and all the variations in between.

The earth

The different kinds of weather we experience are driven by atmospheric pressure. It is the movement of blocks of air around the earth, as atmospheric pressure changes, that causes the changes in the weather. Some of these movements happen on a global scale. The sun is warmest around the equator. The warm air here rises causing a belt of low pressure. At the North and South poles the cool air sinks, making these areas of high pressure. Because the air is moving in these three regions, there are plenty of secondary currents of air in between the two.

The continental masses of land warm quickly in summer, causing the air to rise and low pressure areas to form. In winter these masses cool quickly too, cooling the air and creating pools of high pressure.

These processes interact with the rotation of the earth to create global weather systems. Wind is the experience of air rushing from high pressure areas to low pressure areas. Because the earth is a rotating sphere, the flow of air between blocks of high and low pressure is also caused to rotate so weather maps will often show rotating masses of air moving across the land or the sea.

Weather maps often show isobars – like contour lines, only linking together areas of barometric pressure. The closer together the isobars are, then the faster the air will be moving from high pressure to low, so the higher the wind speeds will be. A depression is an area of low pressure.

Where does it come from?

To understand what sort of weather is heading your way you have to know which direction the mass of air is coming from. In the northern hemisphere, air coming from the north is cold; air coming from the south is warm. This is reversed in the southern hemisphere. Wherever you are, air blowing over land tends to be drier, air blowing over sea picks up moisture. And the more sea it crosses the more moisture it collects. In summer, air which has blown over a large land mass will be warm. In winter,

air blowing over the same land mass will be cold. Things are a bit more complicated in the Pacific rim, especially Australia, where the climate is affected by large changes in seawater temperature caused by currents in the Pacific Ocean and known as El Niño. That's more than we can explain here!

So when you see a weather map (they are known as synoptic charts) and it tells you which way the weather is moving, you have a reasonable chance of predicting its outcome when it reaches the hills you are heading for.

Frontal systems

The boundary between two masses of air is known as a front. In the Atlantic, the warm wet air from the southwest collides with the mass of cold air in the north and east in the Polar Front. As the two air masses slide past each other, little eddies or depressions spin off. These form the frontal systems familiar on weather maps in the UK.

There are three characteristic phases to a moving frontal system.

The warm air mass rises within the frontal system and the cold air rushes in underneath it. As it rises it cools and reaches its dew point. At this point it usually starts to rain, the clouds and rain being most heavily concentrated at the two zones of impact – the warm and cold fronts. Because these are dynamic weather phenomena, if you stand in one place for long enough you'll see the whole sequence played out above your head over time.

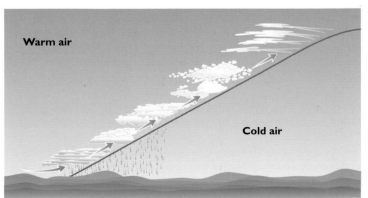

A **warm front** is the leading edge of a mass of warm air.

Warm air

Cold air

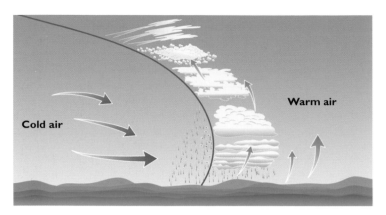

A **cold front** is the leading edge of the mass of cold air that follows the warm air.

Cold air

Warm air

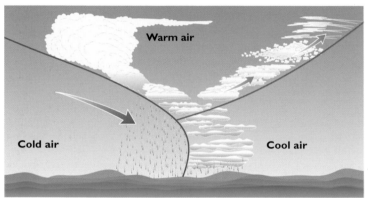

An **occluded front** is the result of the cold front overtaking the warm front and wedging in between the surface and the warm air.

Warm air

Cold air

Cool air

And in the mountains

Warm air absorbs water vapour, like sugar dissolving in hot coffee, but there is a limit to its capacity. When this limit is reached the air is said to be 'saturated'. The higher you climb, the lower the atmospheric pressure, so when air rises in the mountains, it expands (there is less pressure to hold it together). When any gas expands, it also cools. So when moist air moves over hill country, it is forced to rise, and in doing so it is cooled. As it cools its ability to carry water vapour decreases. Its saturation point is lowered and the vapour begins to condense in clouds (the dew point). The higher the air climbs the cooler it gets and so the less moisture it can hold. The excess falls as rain (orographic rain). Once it has passed over the hill country, the air is much drier. Areas in the lee of mountainous regions often have a dry climate caused by this 'shadow' effect.

The rate at which the air cools as you get higher is known as the lapse rate and it depends on how saturated the air is. Moist air cools at a lower rate than dry air. In damp conditions the lapse rate is about 0.5°C (1°F) for every 100m (328ft) climbed. In dry conditions the lapse rate is around 1°C (2°F) for every 100m (328ft). So if the forecast temperature for the nearest town is 8°C (46°F), but you are going to climb to 800m (2,625ft) above that, on a dry day you can expect the temperature at the summit to be around freezing – 0°C (32°F). If you're not sure about the moisture content of the air when you're planning your walk you can use the standard lapse rate – an average based on the two extremes that comes out at around 0.7°C (1.2°F) per 100m – to predict the likely temperature on the summit. You can also use this to estimate where you're likely to encounter snow, and if you learn more about avalanches (which you should — check out one of the avalanche information sites on the web) you can make predictions about the likelihood of avalanches in prone areas.

In the wind

Mountains are colder than valleys and plains. They are also windier. Unfortunately there is no handy rule like a lapse rate to calculate just how much windier they are, but if you look at wind speed records you'll see what the effect of altitude can be. In the UK the highest wind speeds recorded are those from the Cairngorm plateau in the Scottish Highlands. In the US, Mount Washington in New Hampshire claims the highest recorded wind speed in the world, ever, outside a tornado (it's not particularly high by mountain standards, but its north-easterly position and the shape of the surrounding White Mountains serves to accel-erate winds, especially the fierce south-easterly that reached 370km/h (231mph) in 1934).

A lot of this is to do with the funnelling affect of valleys, ridges and cols. But mountains can cause wind speeds to slow down too, by dividing up air flows and, as a result, lessening their impact.

Lightning

Of all the hazards that can beset you on the hill, it is certain that being struck by lightning is one of the most terrifying. That bolt from the blue can zap you without warning melting your boots to your feet and reducing you to a smoking heap. And it's so hard to get away from, too — especially if you're high up or in a forest. Well that doesn't have to be the case. One of the reasons why you should take an interest in the weather around you is so that you can avoid being on that knife-edge ridge in a thunderstorm.

Warning signs

Your best source of information for thunderstorms and the menace of lightning is the weather forecast. And if storms are predicted for your area, amend your plans – it's better to spend a few hours in the outdoor shops. If you do get caught out, there are a few steps you can take to avoid becoming toast. If you hear thunder or see lightning, don't hang around for the rain to come, get to safety as quickly as you can. If you can hear the rumble of thunder the storm is probably only 10–16km away (6–10 miles). You can see lightning a lot further off, usually up to 24km (15 miles) away, but in the hills your visibility and the sound of the thunder may be obscured and deflected by valleys and ridges. When you see the flash start counting. Stop when you hear the bang. Divide your result by 3 for a metric answer and by 5 for a distance in miles. If your result is between 5 and 8km (or 3 and 5 miles), you are in the usual strike zone for lightning, and therefore most at risk.

Protect and survive

The best places to shelter from the rain are often the worst places to avoid lightning strike. Tall trees are natural lightning conductors, but caves and overhangs too will conduct electricity around you and your body will act as a conducting core. If you're in a forest, see if you can find a patch of younger trees. If you're on rocky terrain, see if you can find a boulder on top of another boulder. Sit on your rucksack with your head down and your hands on your knees. You don't need to throw out all your metalware – lightning has bigger fish to fry than be drawn by your ice axe, walking poles, camera or crampons – but it may be sensible to lay them to one side. The middle of a well-drained slope is probably the best place to be.

Clouds

If you take a little time to learn which clouds are associated with the different types of approaching weather you can impress your

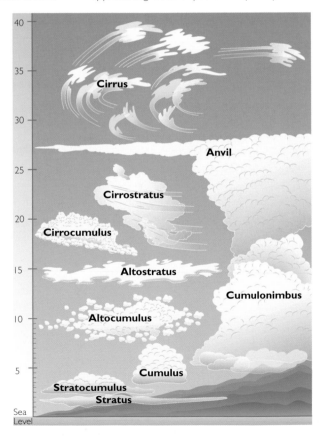

friends with your forecasting prowess on the hill. The basics are shown here. If you only learn to identify two – learn cirrus, the high level, wispy clouds that precede a warm front and follow a cold one, and cumulonimbus, the angry thunderclouds which foretell severe weather.

Wind speed (km/h)	Temperature (degrees Celsius)						
	-25	-20	-15	-10	-5	0	5
5 km/h	-30	-24	-19	-13	-7	-2	4
10 km/h	-33	-27	-21	-15	-9	-3	3
15km/h	-35	-29	-23	-17	-11	-4	2
20km/h	-37	-30	-24	-18	-12	-5	1
25km/h	-38	-32	-25	-19	-12	-6	1
30 km/h	-39	-33	-26	-20	-13	-6	0
50 km/h	-42	-35	-29	-22	-15	-8	-1
70 km/h	-44	-37	-30	-23	-16	-9	-2

Source: Meteorological Service of Canada Wind chill calculator

Wind chill

However cold the air temperature actually is, you will feel colder if there is also a wind blowing. Wind chill is the dramatic factor loved by news reporters because it sounds so dramatic: 'Although the air temperature was just above freezing, wind chill on the remote farm saw temperatures plummet to –10!' There can be no doubt that wind chill is a killer – it's a measure of how your body reacts to the conditions of cold air being blown against it. Freezing air will cause you more harm faster if it hits you at 50km/h! From the chart above you can see that if the ambient temperature is –5°C (23°F) and there is a 20km/h (12mph) wind blowing, the temperature will feel to you as if it is more like –12°C (10°F).

How does this affect the hillwalker?

You have to be prepared for the conditions you'll find in the hills. It's not just a case of checking to see if it's going to rain. High winds can make ridge walking very dangerous. Snowfall can occur even in summer at altitude, rain will swell watercourses making route changes necessary, and poor visibility will slow you down, even if your navigation is Exocet-like. The moral is, keep your eye on the weather reports before you go. Get accurate forecasts, and understand how they will affect you on the ground in the hills.

Skills

So you have the right jacket, the best boots, the most comfortable 'sack. You're fitter than you've ever been and the weather forecast is for clear blue skies. You know exactly where you're going to go and what you're going to eat, but… what are you going to actually do when you get there? Hillwalking is a relatively simple pastime, but there are some core skills you have to know if you're going to enjoy yourself. Good navigation is the key to safely unlocking most of the difficulties the mountain environment can throw at you. Don't skimp on the basics though, or you won't get out of the car park. How you actually walk can make a big difference to your stamina and help you avoid injury. The walking skills section here will help you get the most out of your legs, and keep you on your feet.

But things can go wrong and you need to be aware of the risks and how to manage situations which are unplanned in a hostile environment. The section on first aid deals with practical solutions to real hillwalkers' incidents, so there isn't much on pretty bandages.

The final two sections here take hillwalking a step further. Overnighting on the hill gives you a sense of freedom unmatched by a night in a boring B&B. String a few camps together and you are backpacking like a veteran. While most of this book is aimed at summer conditions, the final section looks at how a covering of snow and ice can dramatically alter things. There is new equipment to handle and new techniques to learn, but learn to master them and you will open up another world of mountain exploration.

■ Navigating without your compass

You don't need to spend three weeks in an ashram in India eating rice and chanting to gain a little direction in life. You do need a map, a compass, a watch and a little bit of know-how. Before you even pick up a compass, you can learn to navigate with GPS-like accuracy by using map and watch alone. In fact good mapwork, not good compass-work, is the keystone of successful route-finding: if you always know where you are from relating your map to the ground, you'll never even need to get the compass out of your pack.

With good navigation skills come safety, freedom and a consideration for the environment. But there's an assumption that good navigators use compasses all the time. That's not true. The better your navigation gets, the less you'll have to rely on your compass, and the more you'll enjoy your time spent in the hills.

Before you go out

A stitch in time saves an unnecessary climb. Spend some time with your map on your living-room floor the night before you go walking. Ignore the strange looks you'll get that night; it'll be worth it when you do get outside.

Spend a couple of hours with maps indoors before you even go out on the hill. You should look at the key and refresh yourself as to what the different symbols mean. Familiarize yourself with basic contour features. What is a hill, what is a valley, what is a contour? Remind yourself what's a right of way, what's a field boundary. Check that there is legal access where you want to walk, even if there is a path marked across it.

Prepare yourself: sometimes finding the start of the walk can be the hardest part of the day.

Navigation tool kit

Map Whether it's Ordnance Survey (OS), USGS, IGN or even Tasmap, 1:25,000 or 1:50,000, this is the single most important item you take with you into the hills. You'd quite literally be lost without one.

Map case Unless your map is laminated or kept in a waterproof map case, it'll turn into a lump of unreadable papier mâché the first time it encounters rain. Fold your map to show the right bits before you leave home, and don't wear it round your neck – you'll be garrotted by the first breeze that comes along. The best place to keep it is in an easily accessible pocket.

Watch Knowing how long you've been walking for is absolutely vital to successful route-finding. A watch is just as important as map and compass.

Compass In bad visibility, you'll be relying on your compass. It's best to have luminous dials, two-degree markings and a big baseplate. The Silva Type 4 is the time-tested choice.

Headlamp If you forget your torch and it gets dark, you may as well sleep under your map, because it's not going to be of any other use. Take the battery out to make sure your torch doesn't turn on accidentally in your pack, though.

Choice of maps

Some maps, such as Harvey's in the UK or Rando in France, are designed specifically for walkers. The contour lines and paths are very clear. Some are shaded to let you know how easy the terrain is, and some are waterproof. The disadvantage is that they tend to cover only the popular walking areas.

British Ordnance Survey, USGS, IGN and Australian state maps are more comprehensive in their coverage, but are designed for all users, not just walkers. In England and Wales, newer maps show access land for walkers, but older ones don't.

Map scales

Many general purpose maps like the OS Landrangers, which cover all of Britain, are at a scale of 1:50,000. That means that a feature on the map is 50,000 times bigger on the ground. So 2cm on your map is 1km (1¼in to 1 mile) over the ground. They give a good idea of the bigger picture of the lie of the land.

Specialist walkers' maps like Harvey's maps can be at a scale of 1:40,000. So 2.5cm on your map is 1km over the ground (1in is 1½ miles). They give a good bigger picture, but often their coverage is limited to specific areas.

OS Explorer, IGN Série Bleue, Ordnance Survey Ireland Specific Area maps, as well as most Harvey's Superwalkers, are at a scale of 1:25,000. So 4cm on the map is 1km (2½in is 1 mile) on the ground. This means they show double the detail of the Landranger and show field boundaries (fences and hedges), which is useful in farmed areas. However, they can be more confusing and you'll need to carry more of them to cover the same area. In the US there are 54,000 USGS 1:24,000 scale (2.64in to the mile) maps covering the co-terminus states and Hawaii!

Map symbols

On every map is a key showing what the different symbols mean. Study this before you go out to familiarize yourself with the map you're using, especially if you are switching between map publishers, or between old maps and new. Particularly, check contour lines, paths and access markings.

What is a contour?

Contours are the brown lines that cover the map. Each one indicates a constant elevation as it follows the shape of the landscape – like a bathtub ring showing where the water

level used to be. Being able to picture the shape of the land from looking at the contours on a map is the single most important skill in successful navigation. On most fully metric maps there is a contour line for every 10m of height, and a bold one every 50m, but this should be checked on each individual map's key.

Col (pass)

At right are some common mountain features as they appear on the map and on the ground.

Ridge

When you are out
Setting the map
The most important thing to learn how to do is 'set the map'. That means orienting it to north. Identify a big feature that you can see like a summit, and use that to set the map. If in doubt, use the compass. Remember the top of the map is north, so plonk your compass on it, then turn both until the red arrow points to the top of the map.

Crag

The map represents a plan of the ground. So if you mark your position as the central point on the map, all the features you can see around you are in the correct relative positions. You can draw a line on the map from where you are to where you want to go, and it'll point the right way over the ground.

V-shaped valley

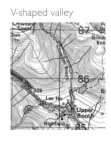

With an oriented map, the landscape around you falls into place. Then you can identify all the features you can see and pick a route cross-country towards an objective you can't yet see.

Estimating distance and time
Working out how far away your destination is, and from that how long it'll take you to get there, are vital skills. First, it means that you can choose a day out that suits your needs; and second, it helps you find your way: if you know that the path junction you are looking for is 15 minutes walk away, you have an important tool to help you find it.

Estimating distance from the map

Each map is covered in grid squares, and each square is usually a kilometre. If you can remember your school maths, Pythagoras tells us that the diagonal of each unit square measures 1.414. So when you are eyeballing longer distances to work out how far you're walking over a few hours, you can count the number of squares crossed lengthways as 1km (⅔ mile), and the number crossed diagonally as 1.5km (just under a mile).

For more precise measurements, use something flexible like a compass string or a piece of grass. Lay it along the path you want to measure, then use either the ruler on your compass or the scale on the map to find out how far it is.

EXERCISE

When you're out on any walk, pick out a prominent feature you can see like a peak, a stream junction or a building. Guess how far away from you it is. If it's a peak, guess how high it is.

Now get your map out, identify the feature and measure how far away it really is. This is a great exercise. It gets you used to relating what you can see back to the map, and makes you much better at judging distances.

Up or down?

Looking at contours, it can be hard to tell which way is uphill, which is down. The easiest way to check is to look at streams and rivers. Small streams flow down into bigger ones. If there are no streams look for a named peak.

Estimating how long it'll take

In the mountains, several factors affect your walking speed: distance, steepness, terrain, fitness and how heavy your pack is. An unfit person carrying a heavy pack uphill in snow is going to make very different progress from a fit walker cruising along a broad ridge on a bright sunny day.

Only experience will tell you what speed you walk at, and this is something to practise; but a good place to start for a normal hill-day

is: 4km/h (2.5mph) plus one minute per 10m contour climbed.

As you get more practised, you'll learn at what speed you can walk in different conditions, and how quickly you can climb 10m (33ft) vertical – a fit walker may only need to add 45 seconds per 10m contour. With heavy packs and a slow group, though, it's more likely to be 90 seconds per 10m.

Writing a timing chart like the one below on your map or a piece of card saves you having to do any maths when you're out and about. Don't forget to add on the extra for the climbs, though.

Distance (metres)	Estimated walking speed (km/h)			
	2	3	4	5
100	3 min	2 min	1.5 min	1.2 min
200	6	4	3	2.4
300	9	6	4.5	3.6
400	12	8	6	4.8
500	15	10	7.5	6
600	18	12	9	7.2
700	21	14	10.5	8.4
800	24	16	12	9.6
900	27	18	13.5	10.8
1000	30	20	15	12

EXERCISE

What's your favourite mountain day? Get your map out, and work out how long it should take you to walk in good conditions carrying just a daypack. Get in the habit of doing this the night before you go on a walk, and you'll soon become accurate.

With exercises like this, you don't even need to be out to improve your skills. Practise in the comfort of your living-room and you'll make sure you can get it right before you venture outdoors.

Handrails

Walking in the hills, most of us follow paths most of the time. Any linear feature like a path, stream or ridge that can be walked along is known as a handrail feature. When you're trying to work out where you are on the map, these are a big help: for example, if you know you're somewhere on the path between Boggy Bottom and Howling Hill, all you need to do is work out how far along it.

Ticking off

The best way to make sure you stay on track is by breaking your day up into short stages. Try to make sure your route links up easily-identifiable features that aren't too far apart – say, every 500m (547yd). When you hit the feature you are expecting, you can tick it off and start the next leg, confident of your new position. And the shorter each stage is, the less chance you have to make a mistake.

So you might follow a path to the foot-bridge (tick), then continue to the tarn (tick), climb to the ridge (tick) and so on.

Collecting features

Sometimes you can't find a feature to tick off at the precise point where you need to turn off the ridge you're on, or start heading east to pick up another path. But what you might be able to identify is a collecting feature. This is one that lets you know when you've gone too far. For example you might have to turn off a ridge 200m (219yd) before reaching the little tarn. So if you hit the tarn, you know you've gone too far.

EXERCISE

What's the route you most aspire to? Out with your map, and try to break it up into as many short legs as you can. Ideally each leg will be no longer than 500m (547yd), and if you can't tick off a feature at the end of one, try to identify a collecting feature as back-up.

With a bit of preparation, you'll find that what used to seem impossible now seems manageable. Don't be scared of getting lost; get out and give navigation a go.

Expert's tip

Buy laminated maps. They're more expensive, but it can be a false economy to buy the unlaminated ones, as they won't last more than a few days of hill use. And the waterproof ones make a great seat! With a stiff new laminated map, carry a hair bobble or an elastic band to hold it folded how you want it. Then slide the band along the map to mark your position. You can often get maps laminated for you by specialist map suppliers if there isn't an off-the-shelf laminated version.

Skills

Navigating with your compass

There's not a lot that you can really rely on in this world. Advertising executives, inventors of slimming products and used car salesmen are all out to bamboozle you. But you can always rely on your compass. However thick the cloud, however dark the night, the little red arrow always knows the way to the magnetic North Pole.

A compass is for when your eyes and the map alone aren't enough. There are three instances when you might use one in clear conditions: when bad weather is sweeping towards you and you want to get a quick fix on your position; when you're moving cross-country on an off-trail route; and if you're on a long stretch of featureless land, and something easily identifiable pops up.

But the mountainous regions can get very claggy. And when the cloud descends or darkness falls, it's time to whip out your compass and find your way safely to your destination.

Navigation tool kit

Direction of travel arrow
Once you have set the bearing, this indicates the direction that you need to follow across country.

Scale ruler
Use the longer scale to measure the distances on the map which are too big to measure with a romer scale. It's useful to memorize a few quick conversions, which become second nature. For example, on 1:25,000 maps, 4cm equals 1km; and on 1:50,000 maps, 2cm equals 1km.

Stencil holes
Allow you to make exact position markings on the map.

Calibrations
The compass housing is marked in calibrations of 360 degrees with 2 degrees graduations. Some are also marked in 'mils' for military use.

Silicone feet
These stop the compass sliding around on the map when you want to take a bearing.

Magnifier
For reading detail on the map. This feature is larger on orienteering models.

Romer scale
Should have both 1:25,000 and 1:50,000 scales for measuring between points on the map, and for working out a six-figure grid reference.

Index line
The point at which the bearing is read off. This is luminous on some models.

Luminous points
To follow a bearing at night, you need one on the needle, and one on the direction of travel arrow. These glow under torchlight.

Orienting lines
You set these in line with the north–south grid lines on the map when taking a bearing.

Clear base plate
You need a large base plate, long enough to lay on the map between the points that you want to navigate to and from, and also long enough to allow you to line up features on the ground. Rounded edges allow it to sit comfortably in your hand.

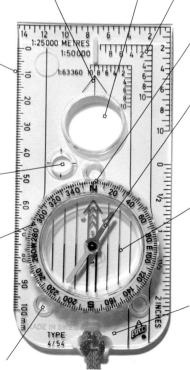

Taking a bearing from the map

You need to get from a summit to a path junction, but the cloud's down. To ensure you're going the right way, it's best to take a bearing from the map, and follow it.

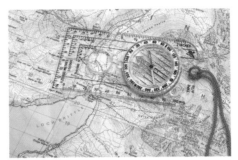

1 Put the compass on the map, placing the long edge on a line from your summit to the path junction. Make sure the direction of travel arrow points from where you are to where you want to go. Check that it will be safe to walk along this line.

2 Keeping the base where it is, twist the dial until the red and black orienting lines are exactly parallel to the north–south grid lines on the map (with the red lines facing north).

3 Your grid bearing is now on the index line. Add some degrees for magnetic variation (see the magnetic variation section at right for an explanation of this).

4 Hold the compass against your body between your belly button and your chest, with the direction of travel arrow pointing forward.

5 Keeping the compass still, rotate your whole body until the red needle (red Fred) lies inside the orienting arrow (his shed, so you are putting red Fred in his shed).

6 Now follow the direction of travel arrow along your bearing to your destination.

Keep the compass still and rotate your body to find the direction of travel.

Expert's tip

When you're taking a bearing, always think to yourself: 'Should I be heading generally north, east, south or west, and does my bearing reflect this?' At some point, every navigator finds they've taken the bearing the wrong way, and they're 180 degrees out.

by 2009. Outside Britain it is different again. In the Alps variation is negligible, but in Seattle, for example, it's 18 degrees east. The best advice is to look on the local map if you're not sure.

Places a compass won't work

In a very few places, naturally occurring magnetic rocks will affect your compass, for example on the Cuillin Ridge on Skye or Bow Fell in the English Lake District. In these two places, your compass should not be trusted on its own.

Metal objects close to a compass, like ice axes, metal watches and tins of food, can also affect readings. Taking a bearing standing on an iron bridge can really mess things up. Even worse are electric fences and overhead power lines. Make sure you're at least 30m (33yd) away from them.

Magnetic variation

Your compass needle's red end points to magnetic north. British maps are set to grid north, so that all north–south lines run parallel to the 2 degrees W line of longitude. Because the magnetic North Pole scoots around Canada's Queen Elizabeth Islands, over 800km (500 miles) away from the North Pole itself, at the moment magnetic north lies about 4 degrees west of grid north.

So when you take a bearing off the map in Britain, you must add 4 degrees to follow it over the ground. Conversely, when you take a bearing of something you can see on the ground, you must subtract 4 degrees when plotting the bearing on your map.

This all sounds very complicated, but there are various aides-memoire to help you remember what to do. Here are a couple:

- Grid to mag, add. Mag to grid, get rid.
- The land is bigger than the map, so if you're moving from map (grid) to land (magnetic), make the bearing bigger by adding 4 degrees.

But remember, the British figure of 4 degrees is decreasing. It should be 3 degrees

Bad weather techniques

Now you've taken your bearing, you need to follow it accurately. This can be difficult, especially if you're traversing a slope, or if there's a strong side-wind.

If you are good at taking bearings, you might be accurate to within 3 degrees. Then if you're good at following bearings, you might stay within 3 degrees of the compass. So even a good navigator might be working with a

6 degrees error. This works out at just over 10 per cent – so on a 500m/yd leg, you are 52m/yd out.

If you're a little bit less accurate, your error could easily be double this, meaning that on a 500m/yd leg, you would end up 104m/yd away from your desired destination.

Following a bearing

The best method is to pick out a feature on your line of travel like a boulder, walk to it, pick a new one, walk to that, and so on. That way, you won't drift to one side without realizing it.

The problem is that in bad weather, you often can't see very far. So the best method is to ask someone else to walk in your footsteps 10m/yd or 20m/yd behind (depending on visibility). Have a third person walk along the same distance behind them, with a compass showing the same bearing as you are follow-ing. Make sure the third person is within your range of visibility from the front. As you walk on your bearing, the third person can sight along their compass through the second per-son to you, and they will see clearly if you are drifting off to one side or another.

If there are only two of you or you've only got one compass, you keep the compass and send the other person out in front. You then advise them to move left or right to make sure they're on the exact bearing. The disadvantage

of this is that it is slow, and involves sending less experienced members ahead. If two of you have compasses, you can speed it up by 'leapfrogging' each other.

Aiming off

To avoid missing your target and not knowing which side of it you are, a good technique is to 'aim off'. For example, if you're aiming for a footbridge over a stream, take your bearing for a point 100m/yd upstream of the bridge. That way, when you reach the water you know you'll have to walk downstream to find it.

If you get lost

It doesn't matter how good you are at naviga-tion, if you're moving through unfamiliar terrain, you won't always know exactly where you are.

To prevent this, keep the legs short, verify your position wherever possible, and keep an eye on your watch. That way even if you get confused, you know that you have to be within a certain distance (based on the timing) and a certain direction of your last confirmed point.

On the other hand, if you start seeing things you're not expecting, or you fail to find something you are expecting, stop and get your map out immediately. Look at the features around you and try to work out where you could be. If visibility is bad, don't stand still. Try walking in a known direction for a measured distance until you see a feature you can identify.

Counting paces

In the previous section we showed how timing your navigation legs can allow you to estimate how far you're walking. But when the visibility is bad and you're using your compass, you need greater accuracy. The best way of accu-rately measuring distance is by keeping the legs very short – less than 300m/yd – and counting your paces. Like timing, practice makes perfect. So measure 100m/yd stretches when you're out walking, and count how many double paces they take you over different terrain and steepness. 'Double paces' means counting every time your left foot hits the ground; it's easier than counting every single pace. It'll be different for everyone, but the chart below is a good place to start:

Double paces per 100m (109yds)			
	Terrain		
Incline	Good	Moderate	Poor
Flat	65	69	80
Uphill	78	85	100
Downhill	73	75	84

Taking a bearing from the ground

Sometimes in bad weather, you're following a path and there's a sudden break in the clouds. You catch a tantalizing glimpse of something you recognize off to one side – say a tarn. If you can take the bearing of this tarn, it will show you on the map where you are on the path, and confirm your exact position.

1 Turn your body to face the feature you are taking the bearing of. Hold the compass against your body at belly button to chest height, with the direction-of-travel arrow pointing forwards.

2 Keeping the compass still, twist the dial until the red needle (red Fred) lies inside the orienting arrow (his shed, so you are putting red Fred in his shed).

3 The magnetic bearing is on the index line. Subtract 4 degrees for magnetic variation.

4 Put the long edge of your compass on the map so that the direction-of-travel end lies on the feature you've taken the bearing of.

5 Rotate the whole compass until the red and black orienting lines are parallel to the grid lines on the map. The compass edge now marks a line back to where you're standing.

If you can do this with two features approximately 90 degrees apart, your position is at the intersection of the two lines. This becomes more accurate the more features you use, and the closer to you they are. In good weather, this technique can be used to identify the peaks you can see around you.

The only difference is that you put the long edge of your compass on the map so that the string end lies on your position. Then you rotate the whole compass until the red and black orienting lines are parallel to the grid lines as above. The edge of the compass now marks a line pointing to the peak you are trying to identify.

Searching for a feature

You follow your bearing and count your paces, you arrive at the point where you think you left your tent that morning… and it's not there. In bad visibility, this is a common problem; and with the errors outlined above it doesn't mean you're a bad navigator.

Sweep search: To find the feature you're looking for, spread your party out in a line abreast, with each person just within the range of vision of the next, and 'sweep' towards your target. If you don't find it on the first sweep, move over to cover a parallel strip on the return, and so on.

Box search: If you're out alone, you can't do a sweep search. So when you reach your point to start searching, walk north however far you can see (say, 10m/yd). Then head east 10m/yd, south 20m/yd, west 20m/yd, north 30m/yd, and so on in a widening 'spiral'.

Navigation

Expert's tip

If you're going somewhere where it's notoriously difficult to find your way, work out certain bearings beforehand. For example do one from a summit to a watershed you intend to descend by. Doing this in the comfort of your living-room and writing it down on your map, you save yourself a lot of work when you're out on the hill, potentially in bad conditions.

Bearings and pacing

EXERCISE – BEGINNERS

Pick a number between 0 and 120. Use it as a bearing and pace it out for 100m/yd. Then add 120 to it and do the same again. Then add 120 to that, and do the same yet again. You should now be back where you started, having paced out a perfect triangle. Once you've become good at this, try it on a hillside.

EXERCISE – ADVANCED

Pace 25m/yd north, then 25m/yd east. Now pace 50m/yd south, then 50m/yd west. Double it again and go 100m/yd north and 100m/yd east, 200m/yd south, then 200m/yd west. You've walked out from your starting point on a square spiral. Retrace your steps, and see how close to your start point you end up. Most people end up nowhere near. These exercises are really good for accuracy in following bearings, and measuring distances through pacing. If you get good at it, change the terrain, and make the legs longer.

Staying on course in poor visibility

If you are in poor visibility it is much harder to stay on course. One good way of accurately following a bearing is to use the 'leapfrogging' method. Here you set your compass bearing, send a companion ahead and get them to line up with the red point of the compass by asking them to move left or right. You can then

Expert's tip

Go out on a walk you know, so that getting lost isn't an issue. But take your map, watch and compass with you, and do the walk as though it's thick fog or the dead of night. Identify every feature you see, and break the walk up into as many short legs as possible. Follow bearings and count paces, time distances, practise everything until you're really comfortable with it. Then you can take it out on to the hills with confidence.

walk towards them and start the process again.

In high winds it can be difficult to communicate over a distance so it might be better for you to get your friend to stay where they are, while you walk on ahead. When you have walked to just within visibility range, turn round and move yourself left or right until you are on course. To do this, point your compass away from you and, without altering the bearing, line up the white end of the needle with the N on the compass housing. This is known as a 'back bearing' and it overcomes the problems of trying to communicate over a distance in howling wind and winter conditions.

You can also use this technique to check your bearing by turning around to face your footprints. Point the compass in the direction of your tracks, and if you are walking on course, the white end of the needle should be pointing to the N on the compass housing.

If you are off course, move to one side to get yourself back on track, then turn round and continue on your bearing with the red end of the magnetic needle now pointing to the N on the compass housing.

Navigating with GPS

Once you've mastered map and compass skills, you'll appreciate the nifty extra features that a GPS receiver can bring you (see also pages 49–53).

Confirm your position

You'll appreciate this feature if you've ever been on a broad pathless summit, any clues to your exact location blocked out by the mist, wondering if you were about to stroll down the wrong ridge into the wrong valley. Within a few seconds, you can create a waypoint for your current location. This gives you a grid reference for where you are, and by checking your position against the map, you can get down safely.

Routes through featureless terrain

This is where GPS really comes into its own. Crossing moorland on a bearing is one thing, but uneven ground and the lack of features to take a bearing can make this tricky. With GPS, you can set a course for a position, and even if you have to walk around bogs, peat groughs and the edges of woods, the GPS will continue to point towards your waypoint.

Mark waypoints

To enter specific waypoints – anywhere you want to go to – on the GPS, you have to enter the six-figure grid reference for all the features and locations you want to tick off. It's fiddly, so take ten minutes to do this before you set out. Useful waypoints could be path junctions, the start of a ridge or crag that leads to the summit, a summit cairn or the start of the descent path.

You can mark your current position with the click of a button, a facility that is particularly useful if you come across a really good wild camping spot that you want to return to later.

You can call up any of your pre-programmed waypoints during the walk by pressing 'Go To', and the moving arrow on the compass will point to the waypoint, and count the distance back to it.

Routes

A route is a series of waypoints entered in the order you want to navigate them. Press Navigate, and the unit will then guide you along the route. As you reach each waypoint of the route your approach is counted down. When you arrive, the unit starts guiding you to the next one on the list. As mentioned above, the GPS can be 'out' by as much as 25m (27yd). When you arrive, it's an easy operation to reposition the waypoint to avoid any cumulative errors.

Navigation

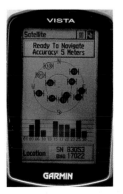

GPS accuracy

In terms of accuracy, the GPS will locate your position to within 10–25m/yd. The way this works on the ground is if you program in a waymarker – a path junction for example – you may reach the junction 10–25m/yd before the GPS says you are due to meet it, or overshoot it by the same distance. Use the map to confirm your location.

In very tight navigation situations the consequences of even slight deviation can be serious. An example is navigating off the summit of Ben Nevis in a white-out. In these conditions, it's vital to note that a GPS is an aid to navigation with a compass, not a replacement. In these circumstances, you should take a bearing from a known location, such as a summit cairn, with a baseplate compass.

Measure your paces

However accurate, bearings are useless unless you can calculate the distance you travel on them precisely when navigating in conditions of poor visibility. Measure your paces and you'll have a safe way of calculating how much ground you cover: it's a skill as valuable as potty training.

1 Identify a relatively flat expanse of open, easy ground on a 1:25,000 scale map such as an Ordnance Survey Explorer. Then look for two easily identifiable landmarks and measure the distance between them. Next, take a bearing from one to the other. For example, from the trig point on the top of Crookstone Out Moor (A) to Madwoman's

Stones (B) gives a distance of 750m (821yd) on a bearing of 76 degrees.

2 Plan a route that takes in this area. Now walk from your identified point A to point B, counting your paces as you go (it's much easier to count a double pace – that is, how many times your left foot hits the ground). Don't march along like an idiot: walk normally, following your bearing.

3 When you return home, calculate the number of double paces you take to cover 100m/yd: (number of double paces you took divided by distance in metres) × 100. The answer should be around 50 to 75 double paces.

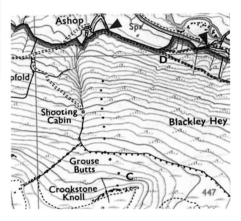

4 Repeat the exercise to measure the number of double paces you take over 100m when travelling downhill, and uphill. Choose an open area with evenly spaced contours: for example, from the point of Crookstone Knoll (C) to the path junction at the bottom of Blackley Hey (D) (a distance of 690m (755yd) on a bearing of 16 degrees).

5 Use a permanent pen to write these figures on a piece of kit you always carry with you, such as your compass. Add five cord locks to your compass cord: when you're counting paces to measure distance for real, slide one along the cord for every 100m/yd-worth of double paces you walk. This enables you to keep count when your brain has all but frozen.

Navigating around the world

The basic techniques for safe mountain navigation are the same everywhere. But there are some important factors to be taken into account if navigating abroad.

Magnetic variation

We all know magnetic north, grid north and true north are very different entities. To navigate accurately, we have to compensate for the difference between magnetic north and grid north. The former is currently located somewhere in Canada's Hudson Bay, but because it moves over time the amount of compensation constantly changes (see page 69).

Mils, grades and degrees

Many topographical maps are prepared by the military. All NATO land forces use mils for angular measurement, so you may find that the magnetic variation is stated in this unit rather than degrees. To use these maps you'll need to know how to convert mils to degrees in order to set magnetic variation.

The symbol for mils is an M with a diagonal line drawn through it and there are 6,400 mils in a 360 degree circle. As with degrees, north is at zero and the measurements are made in a clockwise direction. This means that 1 degree roughly equals 18 mils. So 54 mils of magnetic variation equals 3 degrees.

To further complicate matters, some countries, such as Germany and Switzerland, use a third system of angular measurement, known as the grade. In a 360-degree circle, there are 400 grades, which means that 1 degree equals 1.111 grades. Using this 'conversion rate' you can work out what a magnetic variation stated in grades is in degrees.

Balanced compasses

If you're travelling for long periods in some parts of the world it is worth buying a compass needle that is balanced for the region. A needle balanced for northern Europe and similar latitudes won't settle horizontally if used in the southern hemisphere and tends to scrape along the base of the compass. Companies like Silva can supply compasses balanced for anywhere in the world.

Map grid lines

In the UK, Norway and Canada a grid is placed over the map so that grid references can be used and so that compasses can be set to grid north easily. In other countries grid lines are often not provided or are spaced further apart than expected. Some maps may only have lines of longitude and latitude and these point to true north,

while their wide spacing makes them far from ideal for use with a small compass. The best way around this problem is to draw your own grid lines over the map, by drawing a series of lines that run parallel to the lines of longitude.

Map scale

In the UK, there are maps at 1:25,000 scale for the whole country, but in other countries you may not find such high detail. In most of western Europe 1:50,000 is standard, with larger scale maps available for some countries. But the mountains of Norway are only covered at a scale of 1:100,000. In the US the USGS topo maps are at 1:24,000 but many of the popular recreational areas are mapped at 1:63,360 or 1 inch to the mile. In more remote countries of the world there may often only be smaller scales of map available.

Contours

Contour intervals are not consistent around the world. Indeed, in some countries the contours may be drawn at different intervals on the same map, offering more details on mountain regions where it's needed. Look for a set of contours where heights are provided, and divide the height change by the number of contours to work out the interval. Expect contours to be in metres or feet depending on the country.

Contours may also be drawn in different colours to indicate terrain. In the Alps, for example, areas of grass and earth are indicated by brown contours, rock by grey contours and glaciers by blue contours.

Map shading

Swiss maps are well known for having a three-dimensional appearance. This makes reading of the map very easy, as the map appears almost like an aerial photograph, with ridges and glaciers very clearly indicated. Slopes facing north and west are shaded lighter than those facing south and east.

Detail

The detail shown on maps varies greatly. In the UK the maps show almost every boulder, but in other countries less detail may be available due to inaccurate, scarce or out-of-date surveying. This means navigators have to rely more on contours and basic features. The mapping for some countries is very old, which means that features such as roads, forests and buildings may have changed their shape completely, if they exist at all.

In recent years the effects of global warming have been pronounced. Glaciers have receded and crevasses have moved over time. Make sure you are using up-to-date maps, and be prepared to encounter features or terrain not shown on the map.

Rights of way

The laws on rights of way vary throughout the world with some maps giving detailed information on access, while others provide no information at all. In ski areas winter ski routes may be marked in red, and these shouldn't be confused with summer walking paths!

Sensitive countries

Some countries are very sensitive about anyone who wanders too close to a military installation. These may be sporadically marked on maps, so you should be sensitive to local feelings. On the whole you are likely to be OK using any mapping which is widely available or bought locally, but if you have any doubts as to local restrictions, it is better to consult the national authorities first.

Altimeters

As mountains in some countries are far larger and the distances between obvious features can be far greater than you may be used to, an altimeter can be a useful tool for navigators. It is a basic aneroid barometer which measures air pressure. The pressure decreases as you gain height and increases as you lose height. So, once calibrated in feet or metres, a change in pressure can indicate your height above sea-level. However, as air pressure also changes with the weather, an altimeter must be set at a known height and checked when you reach a known altitude.

GPS receivers

Poor mapping coupled with the vast, featureless terrain of some mountain regions makes navigation very difficult at the best of times, so a GPS (Global Positioning System) receiver is often worth using. These palm-sized devices are an ideal assistant when navigating, but they don't work well in dense forests, such as those in North America, as the trees block the receiver's view of the satellites needed to calculate its position.

Local advice

All the problems stated here mean that up-to-date local information is very important, so it's always worth hunting down the latest editions of maps and guide books and then checking locally if possible.

■ Walking skills

How hard can it be to put one foot in front of another until you get to the top of the hill? And then reverse the process on the way down? Well, that might be the case if we were climbing to the 19th floor, but in hill country the terrain, the exposure and the altitude can all conspire to make your journey a little more taxing. With a bit of thought though, you can prepare your body and your mind to deal with the conditions that you are likely to encounter on the hill.

Make efficient ascents

However fit you are, the speed of your summit bid is dictated by how out of puff you get. Teach yourself to breathe efficiently and your performance on the hill will improve. Mastering the correct technique then training the right muscles is straightforward, but the results are impressive: a fit athlete trained to breathe efficiently will be capable of breathing a maximum capacity of 350 litres (21,358cu in) of air per minute; the average couch potato manages a maximum level of just 50 to 60 litres (3,051–3,661cu in) per minute. So if you only act on one snip of advice from this book, choose this one: it'll make walking uphill a whole lot easier.

1 First, you need to understand how you breathe. Lie on the ground and place one hand flat on your stomach and the other across your chest. Relax and breathe normally.

Now which hand moves most? Most of us find that the chest hand wins the contest. This means that you are contracting and expanding your rib cage muscles to pump air in and out of your lungs. These muscles are just like most other muscles in your body: work them hard and they'll get tired.

2 Try the exercise again, taking deeper breaths so your chest hand stays still and the hand on your stomach moves up and down. Breathing like this also uses your diaphragm, a large muscle at the base of your lungs. This muscle is unique: it contains an almost equal level of fast-twitch fibres (for short-duration power) and slow-twitch fibres (for endurance). This means it's more resistant to fatigue: take deep breaths using your diaphragm when you're walking uphill and you can breathe harder for longer. The result? Far fewer rest-stops to catch your breath.

3 But we're not finished yet. Lie down again, relax and think about what takes the most effort: inhaling or exhaling. Average humans among you will report that breathing in requires the most energy. So try this: take a deep breath and concentrate on exhaling instead, emptying all the air from your lungs. You'll find that your body now automatically triggers another breath: go with the flow and let your lungs be filled with air – it requires much less effort.

4 Try breathing in through your nose: this warms the air before it hits your lungs, so it's less likely to trigger an asthma attack. Now breathe out through pursed lips. This creates a level of back-pressure, which keeps the alveoli (the tiny air sacs in your lungs that exchange carbon dioxide for oxygen) open as you exhale, enabling them to continue extracting oxygen for a fraction longer.

5 The muscles you use to breathe are just like the others in your body: train them and they'll get stronger. Now you won't master this technique overnight – after all, you've some pretty ingrained breathing habits to break – but the more that you

practise, the more natural it will seem and the stronger those muscles will become. Any exercise requiring you to breathe hard (yes, we do mean any) will help your performance on the hill.

Stand straight, walk further

If your hands are free, keep them that way. On the hill, arms are for balance; and if your posture is correct, they will swing freely at your side and do this job just fine. Holding on to your rucksack straps, clasped behind your back and in your pockets are unnatural positions that impede circulation, resulting in swelling or uncomfortable pins and needles. Your arms should be bent at a 90-degree angle when walking, but in practice 50–60 degrees is fine.

Many boot manufacturers design their soles to reflect the expected foot movement; the Scarpa SL, for instance, has a markedly curved sole to roll the foot heel-to-toe as you walk; the smoother your step, the less wear on your shins and ankles, so aim to hit the ground with your heel, roll forwards on to the ball of your foot, then push off from there.

Avoid looking at the floor unless you are on dangerous ground. Keep your head up and towards the horizon at its natural angle, allowing the strong vertebrae to absorb impact and bear the weight of your head which, averaging

about 8 per cent of your bodyweight, is a deceptively hefty burden. If you want proof, relax your neck muscles and gently let your head slump forwards – feel the back of your neck burning? That's muscle being stretched by the weight of your head.

'Sway-back' is an unnatural arch in the

Combine all these methods to take deeper breaths using your diaphragm, with the emphasis on exhaling through pursed lips, and the result is a more efficient breathing technique: you'll use less energy but increase the level of oxygen uptake and carbon dioxide output. There are other benefits too. You may notice the absence of your usual post-walk shoulder and neck pain that you blame on your 'sack. The more likely explanation is that, when you're breathing hard using your rib-cage muscles, you normally recruit the surrounding muscles to support your breathing. And if you're planning any high-altitude trips this year, learning to breathe efficiently is vital: at 5,000m (16,404ft), the amount of oxygen in the air is around half that at sea-level.

lower back; it's common when descending, compounded by a weighty pack, and truly agonising over long distances. Tense your abdominal muscles, pull in your stomach and clench your buttocks – this puts your pelvis into a more 'neutral' position and places your back into a strong posture. Apply this technique on the hill and feel the difference.

The first thing to remember is to stick to shorter, comfortable strides – overstretching can strain your quads, hamstring tendons and calves, and you will feel pulling in the back of the leg and calf if your strides are too long. When descending a rocky path, be careful to keep descent steps small so as not to overstretch. Try to position your knee in line with your second toe as you step.

Coming down

Some skills you simply can't learn in an emergency: making a speedy but safe descent is one of them. It's not a task you'll need to do often; but, should the need arise, it's vital you can do it with confidence. Practise pushing it down a slope on an otherwise relaxed route to hone your technique and you'll minimize the risk if you ever have to do it for real.

Plan your route

Plot your route between visible landmarks and glance up to check you're on target every few strides. It's notoriously difficult to stop when descending on wet grass; so before you start, scan the ground for a slight depression or flat area that will help you to stop safely. By breaking your route into short sections, each with a safe stopping area, you'll reduce the risk.

In an emergency, you should look for stable ground such as fixed rock. However, it's important to practise descending all types of terrain. Duck off the path to rock-hop between boulders; learn how to negotiate wet grass; discover your limits. Keep your knees slightly bent to lower your centre of gravity and absorb shock. Your steps should be short, with your heels biting first. Use your arms to fine-tune your balance.

Test yourself during your

Trekking poles

The extra points of contact poles provide improve your balance, reduce concussion and speed your progress during descent – if you use them well. The most common mistake is holding the poles incorrectly. Place your hand through the strap from below, so the pole hangs from the wrist. Now bring your hand down on to the pole handle. All your weight should be on the strap – you need only have a light hold on the handle to guide the pole into place.

Lengthen your trekking poles before starting your descent – they should be long enough to allow you to place them in front of you without compromising your balance. Use the poles in a natural rhythm with your arms, planting the right pole just before your left foot hits the ground. Place each pole well in front of your leading foot and don't be afraid to lean forwards and load some of your weight into it so it effectively brakes your movement. As soon as your body starts to draw level, flick the pole out again.

Used correctly, for every 6 miles, your poles can save a whopping 1 mile's worth of jarring on your knee joints.

descent. You should be able to stop dead at ANY moment – if you have trouble doing this it's a sure sign you're going too fast. Slow down, work on your balance and you'll naturally improve your speed.

Downclimb with confidence

Most people only downclimb in an emergency – which isn't the best time to discover you can't do it well. The first rule of downclimbing is to make sure you're heading towards easier ground, not getting into even more trouble. Have a good look at the map and identify any difficult sections before you start, so you can visualize exactly where and how you will descend.

On a steep gradient, face the rock. Let your body hang away so you can look down and get the best possible view of the route below.

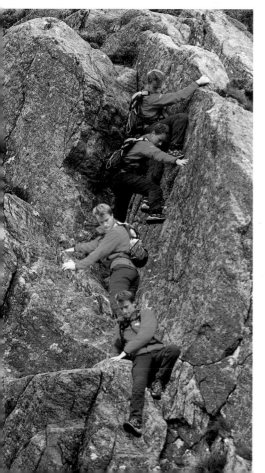

Keep your legs bent and your arms straight, letting your legs take the strain. Don't hang on your arms as they will tire quickly.

On shallower gradients, face sideways to the rock. Move slowly, maintaining three points of contact at all times. Be wary of sitting on your backside and lowering yourself over steeper steps. Your rucksack will push your centre of gravity away from the slope where the ground is most convex – the last thing you want. Once you've spotted your route, turn back to face the rock. Ice axes and trekking poles projecting from your pack can also pose a problem – as can loose straps – so keep your 'sack tidy.

As the ground begins to level out, it's safer, not to mention quicker, to face outwards. It's harder to see your route from this position but look out for polished rock or crampon scratches, or the yellowed line on looser ground, all of which mark a common route. Test hand- and footholds before you transfer your weight and make use of natural foot jams such as gaps between rocks, rather than open, flat surfaces that won't hold your foot in place. Treat patches of steep grass like snow – kick steps with your heel or sole edges. If you get into difficulty, it is best to retreat back up the slope – having several stabs at finding the right descent route is better than going further and further off track.

Deal with scree

The first rule of descending scree is to be cautious. The temptation to run down is strong but, before you commit yourself, make sure you can see the entire length of the scree – this type of broken, monotonous terrain can easily disguise a huge cliff. Break your proposed route into visible sections and reassess after completing each part. Keep your pace controlled and remember that speed not only puts you at greater risk: it also increases erosion.

On some routes you have no choice but to tackle the scree. However, if there is a feasible route that avoids the scree slope, take it: otherwise, your footsteps will accelerate erosion.

Assess the terrain before you begin your

descent. Uniformly sized scree offers a cushioned, safer descent, whereas a hotch-potch of different sized rocks is much more likely to leave you with a sprained ankle. Bear in mind that the depth of scree also varies: if you hit an area where there's only a shallow layer on the bedrock, you're likely to fall. Keep your brain focused during your descent and alter your speed according to the changing terrain.

It's also worth checking out where the gullies – the lines in which the scree falls – are in relation to your line of descent. If you're breaking your descent into sections, make sure that each ends clear of these gullies.

If you're descending as a group, have a chat before you begin your descent and decide how you'll tackle it. It's important that those going first won't be at risk from rocks dislodged by those following. On a narrow scree slope, it's best to stay close together, with the head of the person in front above the feet of the person behind, or to descend individually. Wider slopes allow you to descend side by side, or to zig-zag across the slope (in which case the whole group should re-assemble at each side of the slope before continuing). If you do dislodge a rock, bellow 'Below!' loudly

in order to warn any walkers below you. Don't be sheepish about this. Any embarrassment is easily outweighed by the fact that you might save someone from a nasty head injury.

Keep the weight in your heels and make short but positive steps: it's important that you keep your back straight and your feet beneath you or you'll quickly gain a dangerous level of momentum. Keep your knees slightly flexed to absorb stress and improve balance.

Walking at altitude

The Earth is surrounded by a protective atmosphere, and the higher you climb above sea-level, the lower the air pressure and the fewer oxygen molecules it contains. Be in no doubt: the usual trekking altitudes will take you into potentially seriously low levels of oxygen. To stay alive, your body needs oxygen. It can adapt to a reduction of oxygen, but this is a slow process. Climb faster than your body adapts, and you'll suffer from altitude sickness. Your body can deal with mild altitude sickness for a short period – but if you continue to starve it of sufficient oxygen, you will die.

What is altitude sickness?

Three forms are most common:

Acute mountain sickness (AMS)

This is the first stage, and it's a warning that your body is struggling to cope with the altitude. Symptoms include a headache, fatigue, shortness of breath, appetite loss, nausea, vomiting, dizziness and fainting. Bear in mind you might just experience one symptom, and not all at once.

High altitude cerebral oedema (HACO)

Your brain swells. The symptoms of AMS worsen, and you're likely to experience problems with your balance, mental confusion, an increased pulse rate and hallucinations. These will be aggravated if you exert your body – for example, by walking quickly.

High altitude pulmonary oedema (HAPO)

Normal air pressure stops excess fluid leaking into your lungs, but at altitude, where air pressure is lower, fluid can accumulate. Symptoms include a rapid pulse rate; difficulty breathing; and wheezing, persistent coughing and spluttering. Both HACO and HAPO can be fatal.

Even if you've spent several weeks gradually acclimatizing, don't discount any of the above. Acclimatizing helps avoid altitude sickness – but it doesn't prevent it.

If you get sick

The ultimate answer is simple: descend. If you recognize mild symptoms of acute mountain sickness (AMS), use your judgment: stay at that altitude and you'll probably feel better within 24 to 48 hours. But if any symptoms worsen, or you get any warnings of brain swelling (stumbling or confusion) or lung oedema (wheezing or persistent cough), descend immediately and seek medical attention. Supplementary oxygen will help, but it is not an alternative to descent.

If you do experience mild symptoms of AMS, take your circumstances into account when deciding whether to stay at the same altitude. AMS can turn into HACO or HAPO frighteningly quickly, so you must be confident that you can get yourself out of trouble. Is the descent over easy terrain? How quickly could

you get medical treatment? And above all, remember that a lack of oxygen impairs your judgment: therefore question your decision and always listen to the advice of others.

Help yourself

Consider Diamox (acetazolamide). It corrects the pH of your blood. Nothing works better than time, but if your acclimatization schedule is rushed, then Diamox will help – but it is a diuretic (which means it makes you wee more), so drink lots of water. It's also a prescription drug so ask your doctor for further advice.

Eat a balanced diet before you go. You'll be putting extra strain on your body so ensure it's well stocked with the necessary vitamins and minerals to work efficiently.

Drink plenty of water and steer clear of alcohol. This will help keep your kidneys functioning properly and remove waste products. You'll lose a substantial amount of moisture through over-breathing and sweating so if you're not urinating as often as normal, take it as a warning sign and drink more.

Get fit. The fitter you are, the more efficiently you walk, and the less oxygen you need.

How high is safe?

Recognize that no altitude above 2,300m (7,546ft) is 100 per cent safe, because each individual reacts differently to the oxygen deficiency. Weigh up the risks for yourself using these general conclusions:

- Nearly everyone can safely climb straight from sea-level to 1,500m (4,921ft), then ascend by 300m (984ft) a day to 3,700m (12,138ft).
- All people who climb rapidly above 2,500m (8,202ft) are likely to be affected by some form of mountain sickness.
- Don't forget that the barometric pressure – and thus the level of oxygen in the air – is affected by changes in the weather and temperature. It's not just about height.
- The higher you climb, the slower your rate of ascent must be.
- You simply don't acclimatize above 6,000m (19,684ft).

First aid and emergencies

You come across a body on a ledge below you. The person appears to be unconscious. What should you do?

First aid in the mountains has little to do with triangular bandages, antiseptic and sticking plaster. What really counts is knowing how to react when you're faced with a rescue situation. It's a cool head that ultimately saves lives.

Many instructors talk of giving people a 'sound mental approach' to rescue situations. The aim here, is to teach 'big' first aid, rather than cosmetic first aid. The important thing is to keep people alive and monitor their progress until qualified medical help arrives.

So it's important to keep things simple. There is a logical way of assessing and responding to rescue situations. Managing those situations well is key to saving lives. You don't need to know loads of stuff. Most people only practise their first aid once every three years, so it's difficult to remember lots of tricky procedures.

Follow these guidelines and you will have a good foundation for dealing with any first aid situation in the hills. That ultimately means you could make the difference between life and death for your friends, family and other mountain users.

The first aid kit

There are a number of good first aid kits available on the market. If you want to make your own personal first aid kit, Outward Bound recommends you include the following:

- 6 alcohol swabs
- 1 roll 2.5cm (1in) tape
- 10x10cm (4x4in) gauze pads
- 20x19cm (8x7½in) bulk dressing
- 7cm (3in) gauze roll
- 10cm (4in) elastic bandage
- 10 sticking plasters
- 8x15cm (3½x6in) blister pad or moleskin

- 1 pair examination gloves
- cotton-tipped applicators
- blanket pins
- 1 razor blade
- 1 pair of tweezers
- emergency torch
- lighter or waterproof matches
- knife
- soap
- iodine
- antiseptic

Expert's tip

What most people consider useful first aid items are actually just for personal care and cosmetic purposes. The only life-saving thing that you can carry at this level of first aid is a wound dressing and bandages to stop severe bleeding. Most first aid involves improvization, using the things you usually carry in your rucksack or what you find to hand in a mountain setting. For that reason, a good first aider with no gear at all is of far more use than a bad one with a full kit.

A doctor with years of training and experience can have difficulty making a diagnosis in the cosy environment of their consulting room, so you need to be realistic about what you can achieve. The best thing is to concentrate on what you *can* do, and not on what you can't.

First principles

First aid is all about organized thinking and good management of a rescue situation. When you find someone who's been injured, you need to take time out to assess the situation. If you race to someone's rescue and injure yourself in the process, you've immediately made the situation worse. If you send a hail of scree on to their heads or land on top of them wearing a pair of crampons, you've really made things worse. So you need to think and assess the situation using the following criteria...

- **Personal safety:** If you sustain an injury you immediately reduce your capacity to deal with the situation. Rather than following your instincts and racing down a mountainside, take time to pick a safe route and always approach the casualty from below.

- **Victim safety**: Think about your actions. Is your course of action going to leave the victim better or worse off?
- **Immediate threats**: Deal with the immediate threats to their life first and then tackle those that might arise later.

The ABC of survival

The first thing you need to check is that the basic requirements for life are being fulfilled. ABC stands for Airways, Breathing and Circulation. If the person is talking to you when you arrive then these are obviously already working fine. If they are unconscious you need to check them for yourself.

way is clear and that they are in a safe airway position (see page 86), you'll be one of the finest first aiders who ever walked the hills.

Airways

If a person can't get air into their lungs, they will die in minutes. If they are unconscious and left on their back, 25 per cent of them will die. So if you do nothing else but ensure the air-

Breathing

Make sure that they are breathing regularly and noiselessly. The main worry here is that vomit or blood is entering the lungs, so ideally they need to be lying with their head downhill in a draining position.

Circulation

In order for oxygen to be passed around the body, it is important that there is sufficient blood to carry it. Severe bleeding can rapidly compromise the body's ability to do that. If a patient is wearing layers of waterproof clothing, bleeding can be very difficult to detect. Look for blood pooling in waterproofs as an indication of catastrophic bleeding. To stop bleeding you need to exert direct pressure to the wound. Bare hands or an item of clothing can be used, but a wound dressing and bandage is ideal.

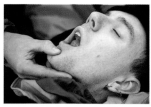

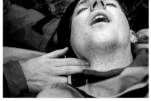

1 Tilt head backwards: the tongue is a massive muscle and you need to move it off the back of the throat to clear the airway. You'll have to move the head back quite a way to make sure you've achieved this.

2 Open the mouth and check for obstructions.

3 Monitor their breathing and keep the airways clear. You can check they are breathing by placing your cheek near their mouth to feel for their breath or, in the cold, actually see the breath.

Get help

If you have a mobile phone and are able to get reception, call for help immediately. Using a map you should be

able to pinpoint your location for the rescue team.

If you don't have a phone then a whistle is a good way of attracting attention – you should make sure you carry one with you every time you go out. Six blasts is the standard call for help. Once you have someone else with you it will make your life four times easier and remove 90 per cent of the decisions you have to make.

Monitor vital signs

If someone is unconscious you need to monitor their vital signs. These tell you how the victim is and whether their condition is improving or deteriorating.

- **Level of consciousness:** use the AVPU scale. This stands for Alert (talking and coherent), Vocal (making some noise but little sense), Pain (only responsive to pain: test this by pinching their ear) or totally Unresponsive.

- **Pulse:** this is normally 60–80 beats per minute. Check this on the nearside of the patient's neck by pushing down two fingers next to the Adam's apple. Some people find it difficult to find a pulse, so get used to looking for other life signs. If someone is breathing there has to be a pulse. Alternatively, pull down the lower lip and check the colour of the skin there. If it's pink, this is a good sign; if it's white there's poor circulation; and if it's blue, no oxygen is getting through.

- **Breathing:** this should normally be 12–18 breaths per minute. If the victim isn't breathing but has a pulse, you'll need to perform rescue breathing on them. If they aren't breathing and they have no pulse, you'll need to perform CPR (see page 93).

- **Temperature:** assess this relative to what might be considered normal in that particular situation.

When to move

Take a 'profit and loss account' approach when deciding on any course of action. For example, if there is a risk of spinal injury but the person isn't breathing, you must clear the airways. If you don't, they'll be dead in minutes.

When not to move

There may be a case for not moving a victim who has fallen into a strange position. You need to think first: 'Is this safe?' Is the airway open and are the lungs draining? If the answer is 'yes', then it may be appropriate not to move them.

Safe airway position

In this position the airways will be free from blockage and the lungs will be clearing, making sure that blood and gunge isn't entering the lungs.

1 Put the patient's nearside hand in the stop sign.

1

2 Bring the other hand over on to the cheek and hold it there.

3 Bring the knee up and turn, keeping their back as straight as possible.

4 Make sure airways are clear and lungs are draining, and monitor breathing.

Detailed examination

When you have ensured that the basic requirements for life (airways, breathing and circulation) are not being compromised you can progress to a more detailed examination. This allows you to gain information to decide on your next course of action. You will also be able to provide the rescue team with this information and tell them how the victim has been progressing. For example: have they been rapidly deteriorating or steadily improving?

Start at the head and work your way down, taking note of any injuries as you go. Only when you have completed the entire examination should you decide which order to tackle them in. Not surprisingly, you will need to deal with the most important one first.

As you examine them, you are looking for obvious injuries, pain or tenderness. Be gentle as there is potential here to cause more problems. The golden rule of first aid is not to leave the person any worse off by your actions.

1 Ask them exactly what happened. This is an excellent way of narrowing down the range of potential injuries they might have sustained. Keep talking to them all the time – it helps to constantly reassure them.

2 Gently check the head and then the neck looking for dislocation and pain or any abnormalities that might suggest an injury. Keep the head still while you're doing this.

3 Check the ears for any blood or fluid that might suggest head injuries. Then check the eyes and mouth. Inside the lower lip is a good place to check the circulation; also look for broken teeth, cut tongue, and so on.

4 Check under the armpits for relative temperature. Hypothermia is a real issue (see pages 90–91 and also pages 121–2) so only undo clothing a little way, then zip everything up once you are finished to maintain heat.

5

6

10

11

5 Check the collarbones for dislocation, tenderness or pain. Then check the shoulders. Use only very gentle pressure; keep talking and reassuring.

6 Check the elbow but be careful never to move an injured elbow as this can cause long-term injuries. So do not bend it but simply look for tenderness and any deformity that suggests injury.

10 Check the pelvis, exerting a gentle downward pressure. Excessive force runs the risk of a fractured pelvis leading to a perforated bladder.

11 Finally, check the hips and thighs and then the knees before moving on to check the lower leg and ankles.

7

8

7 Check the spine by moving your hands gently underneath the back, where you have access to it. If you're not sure about an injury, always assume it exists. That makes decisions much easier.

8 Check the chest, but be very gentle. A broken rib can easily puncture a lung and then you've left the person far worse off than they were before.

9

9 Check the four quadrants of the abdomen. Being able to be specific about where the pain is coming from will help a rescue team.

Patient care

A vital part of managing a first aid situation is talking to the victim and constantly reassuring them. Lots of eye contact, lots of smiling and communicating will have a wonderfully positive effect. When you've stabilized their main life systems (airways, breathing and circulation) you need to get them warm.

Most people who've sustained injuries on the hills talk about how cold they were, rather than the pain of their injuries. So you must maintain their body temperature while you're waiting for assistance. Get them on a sleeping mat, in warm clothing and in a sheltered location. If they're conscious and have sustained no internal injuries then giving them a warm drink will do a great deal to lift their spirits.

Handle with care

Your primary role as a first aider is to keep people alive. When you've done that, it's time to turn your attention to some common hill

injuries. To be an effective first aider in a hill environment, you don't need to know how to treat every ailment you might encounter, just keep things simple and learn the basics.

The first part of this chapter concentrated on 'big' first aid: dealing with breathing and circulation. Without these, a victim isn't going to live long. This next section looks at approaches to multiple casualty situations, and how to deal with some common injuries and medical problems when you're on the trail.

The right approach

When you've ensured that all the requirements for life are being fulfilled – the patient has clear airways and is breathing, their heart is beating and any catastrophic bleeding has been dealt with – there may be other, non-life-threatening injuries that require your attention.

The real killers in the outdoors are unconsciousness, bleeding and cold. Deal with these first before you look elsewhere. When you've done that, you need to do some careful thinking. Look at the victim and ask: 'What are the facts and what do they need next?' Then think 'what daft thing can you do to really mess this up?' and make sure you steer clear of that. Approach first aid in that fashion and you'll be doing a good job.

The golden rule of first aid is to leave the person in your care no worse off than they were before. So you need to think clearly and act decisively. People who do damage are those who aren't thinking things through. They make a mess of things when they don't have full information. If you can't make up your

mind what to do, do only what's essential. This kind of approach makes hill first aid relatively simple and ensures that no costly mistakes are made.

Improvised carries

There are two reasons why you might need to carry a patient before qualified medical help arrives. Either because the situation is very serious or because the injury isn't that serious. For example, if there is a risk of avalanche, you will need to move the person you are looking after to a safe location to prevent further injury. Or, if the injury is very minor, for example a sprained ankle, you might find it easier to get the patient back to a car and drive them to hospital.

Who do you deal with first?

Deal with those in a life-threatening situation first. It's difficult to ignore someone who's yelling at you for assistance, but you need to attend to people in order of risk.

When deciding who to deal with first (if there are multiple casualties), this is the order of priority:

1 **About to die** These people are your top priority; problems include blocked airways and catastrophic bleeding.

2 **Will die soon** These are people with injuries that could prove fatal. Problems include very serious bleeding, which inhibits the body's ability to circulate blood.

3 **Minor injuries** These patients are the least needy, and typically include people with broken limbs. The injury itself isn't fatal but other complications that could arise, such as hypothermia or circulation problems due to fractures, do need to be addressed.

4 **Dead** Sadly, there's nothing that can be done here.

Dealing with bleeding

It's worth remembering that modern outdoor clothing can often make it very difficult to detect bleeding, because blood won't soak through waterproof material. So you will need to look for pooling of blood in the first instance. However, in many cases the source of the bleeding will be very obvious.

Quite often when someone is bleeding they're doing half the job for you. For example they may already be applying pressure to the wound. Your job as a first aider is to finish the job for them: by applying pressure, raising the wound, bandaging it and keeping it raised.

Check circulation

When you've finished bandaging the wound, you need to make sure that the dressing isn't restricting blood circulation. To do this, first grip the patient's hand. Then, when you release it, the colour should quickly turn from white to a healthy pink. If this doesn't happen, there is a risk that you've bandaged the wound too tightly. Loosen and re-bandage the wound.

The importance of warmth

When you've dealt with life-threatening conditions, you need to address the matter of patient care. Especially in maritime climates,

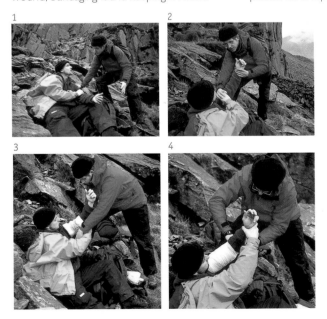

1 Here the casualty is already applying pressure to the wound.

2 Maintain the pressure and raise the arm to reduce blood loss.

3 Apply a wound dressing or use anything which will do the job.

4 Next bandage the wound, making sure that the arm remains raised.

has a broken leg, then 'reduce' the leg (see below) and splint it, because over that amount of time it's going to affect the circulation and nerve functions.

When you're checking the person for injuries a fracture will be detected due to pain, deformity and swelling in any one area.

To deal with a fracture of the leg you need to first reduce the fracture. This is done by pulling the foot to ensure that any sharp bone fragments aren't able to cause further damage. Don't simply pull on the leg; first explain to the casualty what you are doing and why. Applying this traction should reduce any pain they are experiencing.

1

2

1 Reduce the leg by gently pulling the foot away from the body.

2 Now splint the two legs to maintain traction on the fractured limb.

3

4

3 Place a jacket between the legs and part of a sleeping mat under them.

4 Bandage the legs together then test the toes to ensure circulation isn't impaired.

hill weather can mean potential hypothermia, even in summer, although it's almost unheard of now, thanks to modern clothing; but 30 years ago it used to be very common. So while good equipment has removed the threat of hypothermia in healthy walkers, it is still something that you need to address in a first aid situation. Most people who've been rescued talk about just how cold they were, rather than their actual injuries.

So when looking after your victim, you need to prevent them from further cool-ing, insulate them from the cold ground and protect them from wet and wind; and if they are shivering and conscious and haven't suf-fered any internal injuries, give them a warm drink and food. Remember to keep talking to the person. Reassure them and let them know what's going on. Simple patient care is something anyone can do – and the impact is positive and enormous.

Dealing with fractures

Management of people is the key to good first aid. There are times when treatment is all-important. For example if a chopper, isn't going to arrive for four hours and the casualty

1 First loosen any clothing around the neck to ease breathing.

2 If their heart stops, perform CPR (see page 93).

3 Now get the casualty into a sitting position.

4 Raise their legs and try to constantly reassure them.

Heart attack

With increasing numbers of older people discovering the hills, heart attacks are a growing problem. So knowing how to deal with them is important.

Symptoms of heart attack:
- chest pains
- shortness of breath
- sweating
- signs of shock
- anxiety
- blue lips

You need to loosen any clothing around their neck, get them into a sitting position and bring their knees up towards their chest. It is important to get them to hospital as quickly as possible while causing the minimum of stress. So make sure you reassure them constantly and keep them calm.

Head bandage

To deal with bleeding of the scalp, you'll need to stem the flow of blood using a bandage. The important thing here is to ensure the bandage stays on. There are a number of ways of doing this, but an effective method is just giving a little twist of the bandage at the back of the head. Of course good first aid is also about improvization and you can use something like a hat to make sure the bandage stays where you want it.

Spinal injuries

If you're not sure whether a casualty has suffered a spinal injury it's safest to assume they have. That way, you're going to take precautions when moving them and if, when you've got them to hospital, you subsequently find out they don't have any spinal problems, then that's great news.

There are times when you will need to move the casualty, though. Take a 'profit and loss' approach in cases like this. Moving the victim incurs the risk of permanent spinal damage, but if you have to move them, for example to clear an airway, then the benefit of doing so is clear.

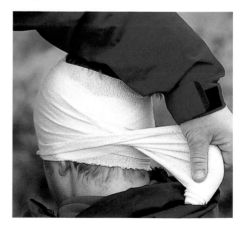

You may need to roll a person with a suspected spinal injury in order to clear their airway. To minimize risk of spinal damage use as many people as possible.

If only two are available, the first needs to keep the head under control, holding it firmly on both sides to keep it in line with the body. The second person should place one hand on the shoulder and one hand on the hip, then roll the victim towards them.

So what next?

This section has given you a good idea how to approach first aid situations, but there is a limit to what a book feature can offer. To practise these skills, or to learn more complicated procedures like CPR (cardiopulmonary resuscitation), you'll need to sign up for an officially recognized course. See page 142 for useful addresses.

Staying out of trouble

Know what to do in a mountain emergency, and your tales of the unexpected should have happy endings.

There are some things you don't have control of – all the 'what ifs' that make life so interesting. One of your party may take it into their head to wander off in bad weather. Out walking alone, you might slip and twist an ankle. Or you might just get taken by surprise by a route that takes much longer to complete than you anticipated.

Follow the advice here, and you'll stop unexpected situations turning into emergencies, and will know how best to deal with the emergencies if they do happen.

To avoid splitting up

To avoid your party splitting up, lay out the ground rules before the walk. If you're with a group of more than five or six, consider appointing a back marker to bring up the rear. That way, when you're leading, you know that if you can see the back marker, the rest of the

group are safely between you and them.

On rough terrain even this is difficult, so in these circumstances make sure you can always see the person behind you. If you can't, stop and wait until you can. If everyone does this, you become linked in a visual chain, which should keep the whole group together.

Danger times

There are particular circumstances in which you're more likely to lose someone:
- descending off a summit
- at path junctions
- when stopping for a rest
- when someone leaves the trail for a pee
- when a path zig-zags
- on scrambles and difficult terrain.

In all these situations, stop and collect your whole group before moving on.

In bad weather

If it is very windy, getting dark, or the cloud comes down, you need to keep a much closer

Your safety tool kit

As well as packing your normal walking clothes, don't venture out into the mountains without these items.

Mountain shelter – These will protect you and your party from the elements in an emergency, yet they are very light to carry

Hat and gloves – For its weight and size, a hat will keep you warmer than any other item of clothing

Map and compass – You'd be lost without them

First aid kit – This is no good to anyone without a little knowledge. Book yourself on a course

Spare food – Always pack even more than usual if you are walking with a diabetic

Headlamp/torch, spare bulb and batteries – If you don't take these, you might have to spend a whole night on the hill

Mobile phone – This may be considered contentious, but it's an important piece of safety kit

Whistle – Everyone should carry a whistle. It will work long after your voice has given out

Skills

eye on each other. Don't be afraid to rein your group in and have everyone stay close.

The lost sheep

Before you set off, agree with everyone that if one person does suddenly find themselves lost and alone, they should stop and blow their whistle. Hopefully someone from the main group will be within earshot. If not, the lost person should retrace their steps to the last point where they know they were with the main group. There, they should put on warm clothes, get out their flask, and put their feet up. If they're not found within an hour, they should head back on their own. As soon as you realize you are missing one of your flock, STOP. Group everyone else and make sure nobody else wanders off. Have a quick look around to make sure the person you are missing isn't just relieving themselves behind the nearest sheep, then start retracing your steps along the path.

Communicate!

If you have a mobile phone, use it to let others know you are safe and well. Don't rely on it in emergencies, though it may prove indispensable if you can get a signal. Head off any false alarms by letting someone know if you change your route or return to a different place.

If you get caught out

No matter how well prepared you are, sometimes something unexpected happens. A route might take a lot longer than you'd calculated, or the weather might make progress dangerous. If so, you're going to have to stay where you are for a while. An unplanned night out in the hills is never going to be the most comfortable of affairs, but it is often preferable to blundering on and making your situation worse. Here's what you need to do:

- find the most sheltered spot
- put on all the clothes you've got with you
- get out your plastic orange survival bag, or your group shelter
- get into the bag or the shelter. If it's a plastic survival bag, you should crawl in head first. This provides the maximum amount of insulation for your head and body core. For safety and comfort, cut a small hole in the corner to aid breathing
- sit on your rucksack to keep yourself insulated from the ground
- have a snack and a drink, and call home to explain that you're going to be late, but you're otherwise OK.

If you have to call mountain rescue

If you think you need rescuing, first consider whether you can help yourself. If there's any way you can drag yourself off the mountain, do so. You don't know when the team will manage to find you.

Before you make any calls to mountain rescue, first ensure you're warm and comfortable by following the advice we've given above.

Next, you will need to decide who does what. If there is no mobile phone reception where you are, try the nearest high spot. Send two people off for help, and ensure someone stays with the casualty. If there are fewer than four of you, either try signalling for help with a whistle or torch (see below), or consider the merits of one person going off to fetch help. But remember, on no account must anyone else get injured. Then write down the following information, which the team will need:

- location: the best way of giving your position is by a full grid reference
- description of the location
- the name of the casualty and their next of kin
- the nature of the emergency, how it happened and the type of injuries sustained

- other members of the party, and the plan of action to be followed
- any relevant information about the terrain and the best approach
- your mobile phone number(s)
- any other relevant medical facts and what equipment you have with you. Before you set out you should check what the procedure for calling out a rescue team is locally as it can differ from state to state and country to country.

Being rescued

When the team gets close, or if you're on your own, you'll want to signal for help. In daylight, this means using a whistle. Six short blasts every minute is the standard distress signal. If it's dark, use your torch to make six flashes. If a helicopter comes to rescue you, make sure the site around you is well marked (if you are in an orange bag, it already is!), but also make sure it is tidy, and there is nothing that could blow around.

■ Camping and backpacking

A few days' backpacking can bring unrivalled freedom. Here's everything you need to make the hills your home.

Organization is the key to a good night under the stars. Backpacking makes you a free agent in the wilderness and keeps you in touch with nature. You get to experience it at its best, woken by sunrises and sudden rainfall…

What to take

When you go backpacking you basically need to take the same gear as you have for day walking, and supplement that with the things you need to sleep and eat. Thinking this way makes it easier to work logically through your kit list to make sure you haven't missed anything essential.

Packing your sack

There's a real art to packing a rucksack because you need to consider a number of factors. Firstly, make sure the items you want during the day are easily to hand. These include

waterproofs, hat and gloves and snacks; keep these near the top of your pack or in accessible pockets. You also need to make sure that your tent, poles and pegs are easy to get to. If you arrive at your camping spot in pouring rain, you want to be able to get the tent up quickly without having to empty the contents of your sack.

But you also need to create little dry pockets in your rucksack. How you do this will depend on the design of your pack. You could use a one-compartment rucksack and a liner to create a dry area at the bottom of your sack. In there put your sleeping bag and any spare clothes. so you know that when you get to camp, they will be dry.

If you're using a rucksack with side pockets, use one as a 'clean' pantry, to store water bottle and walking snacks. Store food and snacks in stuff sacks to make sure they don't get contaminated. Use the other pocket to store your fuel bottle, tent pegs (an item that can easily get lost in your rucksack) and any 'non-edible' items that might contaminate food.

Finally, you want to make sure that you pack heavy items above your centre of gravity and close to your back as this will really improve the stability of your sack. Fold your Therma-rest (or mat) and slide it into the rucksack nearest your back. This gives you extra padding and prevents items digging in while you're walking.

Top of sack
Waterproofs, warm fleece, flysheet, inner tent and poles (broken down)

Left-hand pocket
Water bottle and walking snacks

Top pocket
Hats, gloves, guide book: things you want to hand

Inside lid pocket
First aid kit

Right-hand pocket
Fuel bottle, tent pegs, etc

Middle part of sack
Stove and bulky items like food

Bottom of sack Sleeping bag and dry clothes stored in a rucksack liner

Fitting your sack

A poorly fitted rucksack can quickly make a backpacking trip miserable, so it's worth making sure that yours spreads the load evenly across your shoulders and hips. The first thing to do is to loosen the shoulder straps and ensure that the hipbelt is resting just on top of your hips. You should now adjust the back length so that the straps curve perfectly around your shoulders, then tighten the shoulder straps using the chest height adjusters. Finally you need to tighten the top tensioning straps over your shoulders so as to bring the rucksack in close to your back. This helps

to make the rucksack more secure, and also more comfortable as you're walking.

Using trekking poles

Most people use trekking poles incorrectly. They are really useful for taking some of the strain off your legs, but if you're not using them correctly then you're not going to get the most out of them.

The problem comes from how people use the wrist loops. You need to loop your hands in from underneath the strap and then bring your hand down to grip the handle and the top part of the loop (see pictures below).

When you're adjusting the poles for length, take the bottom section of the pole to the stop line and then adjust using the middle section, as this keeps the end of the pole lighter. Your poles should be roughly at elbow height.

Approach to long walks

When you start walking take things easy at the beginning. Go slow for the first hour to allow

your muscles and heart to adjust. If you've been sitting in the office for the last week, you can't expect your body to leap into action immediately.

If you're walking over a few days, plan in a few rest periods. Take the first day fairly easily: aim to walk gently for no more than six hours with plenty of rests. The second day you can up the pace a little, but on the third day it's a good idea to drop back to the distance you covered on the first day. After that you can pretty much walk as far as you feel able, but do listen to your body.

Food and drink

Have plenty of snacks and make sure you take more than you think you'll need. Spare food is useful for emergency situations (yours or other people's) and you might surprise yourself with just how much your body requires.

Try to eat something every hour and keep drinking at regular intervals. Don't wait until you're thirsty to take a drink; keep sipping water throughout the day. You might find a hydration system built into your rucksack helps you to do this. This allows you to keep taking in water without having to stop and get your water bottle out of your rucksack.. For more food ideas see pages 40–45.

Camping
Finding a good location

There is seldom a right to wild camp, and someone owns every last blade of grass, so officially you need to seek permission to camp anywhere. Responsible camping is generally tolerated in wild areas above the last intake wall – but not everywhere. If you haven't seen anyone camping in that area before it is a good idea to enquire about wild camping at the nearest tourist information centre.

One of the most important things when choosing a place to pitch is to locate yourself near water. Keep yourself away from the path so you're not disturbed by other walkers and look for somewhere that offers some shelter.

Before you settle on a site, try lying down on the ground to make sure that it's comfortable, doesn't slope too severely and isn't water-logged. Soft ground makes it easier to push pegs in and it also makes for a more comfortable night.

Pitching your tent

You want to pitch the tent with the tail facing into the wind, and make sure that you push the pegs in at an angle of about 45 degrees to ensure they stay in the ground. If there is a slight angle in the ground, lie with your head facing uphill. And for comfort you obviously need a roll mat to insulate you from the cold ground.

Dealing with damp

If you arrive at your campsite wet, you'll need to get the tent up as quickly as possible, which is why you have packed it at the top of your rucksack! Flysheet-first erecting tents with hanging inners provide you with shelter quicker but do tend to compromise on space.

If you've packed your dry clothes in a rucksack liner they will still be dry when you've got your tent up. Put these on for the evening to keep warm and leave your wet gear in the porch of your tent to dry out. The following morning, put your dry clothes back in the rucksack liner, so they'll stay dry for the following evening. That means, like it or not, you need to put your damp hiking gear back on.

Getting water

The best source of water comes from fast-moving streams high up in the mountains. You should avoid collecting water from near

livestock, human activity or from still water sources (such as a lake or tarn) or from muddy-looking rivers.

If you have to collect water from anywhere else, make sure you treat it with suspicion. You can either boil the water for 10 minutes (remember to add another minute for every 300m or 1,000ft you are above sea-level), or treat it with chemicals such as iodine (read the instructions carefully). There is a good range of water filters on the market. The very best are water purifiers as these have a microfiltration system to get rid of waterborne particles and a chemical element to deal with viruses and so on.

Bathroom time

Site your toilet downhill from your campsite and at least 60m/yd away from fresh water such as a stream or lake. It should be at least 50m/yd from a path and 200m/yd from huts, crags and caves. Bury your excrement 15–20cm (6–8in) deep (a trowel or ice axe is useful for digging) and either burn or bag toilet paper and take it home with you. Likewise you should bag up sanitary towels or tampons and dispose of them once you get home.

Dispose of water from washing into the

ground well away from lakes or streams and downhill from your campsite.

Breaking camp

When it's time to strike camp you should aim to leave the spot looking untouched. Pick up all your rubbish: this includes apple cores, fruit peel and used matches as they can take years to degrade in a mountain environment. Then replace any dislodged rocks and leave the pitch looking as though you were never there.

Bivying

A night in the hills might not mean a night in a big tent. There are a number of one-person solutions available for those who prefer the ultra lightweight, or perhaps for emergency use. Bivouacking in this way is as much about improvised shelter as camping.

Your choice of site should ideally be flat, well drained but within reach of running water, and sheltered. But think about your chosen site in terms of whether it is a planned or emergency overnight too: if it's planned, then a sheltered spot is a priority; if it's an emergency, you won't have the luxury of searching for a perfect site – and remember that whatever landscape feature you've found to shelter you from the elements could also shield you from the gaze of the mountain rescue team.

But enjoying, rather than enduring, a night in a bivy bag is as much to do with how you get into it as where you pitch it.

Work out a routine before you venture on to the hill: trust us, trying to keep your sleeping bag dry as you get into a bivy bag in the rain is no easy matter. Some folk prefer to strip wet clothes and boots off their bottom half first, then sit in the bag before taking their jacket off. Others prefer to strip off all wet clothes and waterproofs and dive straight in.

Bivy or bothy bag?

Shown right is a survival bag and it's for emergency use only: spend a planned night in this and you'll wake up soaked from condensation. Its main virtues are its price (they are very cheap) and Tango colour – and although it's better than nothing in an emergency, it won't protect you as well as a bivy or bothy bag.

Shown top left on page 101 is a bothy bag or emergency group shelter (or KISU – the Karrimor Instructors Survival Unit was an early variety). You sit inside it and provide the structure yourself. They're light, inexpensive and great as emergency shelters for a group, as they allow everyone to stay together to boost

Look for somewhere that offers some shelter, doesn't slope too severely and isn't waterlogged.   Try to locate yourself near water.   Keep yourself away from the path.

and boots when you're bivy-ing in wet conditions.

Staying in bothies

If camping is not your thing you may prefer to stay in a mountain hut or a bothy. These can vary from the palatial old inns you might find on an alpine pass, to a simple hut with a mud floor and a couple of planks for a bed. Whilst booking is essential in high season for the former, the latter is usually free and run on a first come, first served basis, so you might have to spend your night with several others, not to mention the odd sheep or goat.

body warmth and morale. They are also handy for lunch-stops on cold days.

Shown above, top right, is a bivy bag. It's essentially a waterproof cocoon that you wriggle into, with a vent for breathing. The better models are also breathable (many are made from Gore-Tex) to reduce the level of condensation inside. Good for planned as well as emergency overnight camps.

So which do you need?

The big question is whether you'll only use your shelter for emergency use.

If you're a regular big-dayer, the best option is to invest in both a bivy bag and a bothy bag. While a bivy bag will provide a dependable and watertight emergency shelter, you can also use it for planned overnights, which will bring longer routes within closer reach.

And a bothy bag will earn its keep too. Because it's so light, you won't even notice you're carrying it. It's incredibly easy to get in (unlike the bivy bag) so you can use it as a preventa-tive measure: nip inside for a hot drink and a chocolate bar out of the wind and you'll warm up and feel ready to continue in no time. It also makes a handy cover for your rucksack

Bothy etiquette

Anyone can stay in a bothy: they're not 'mem-bers only'. But abuse the privilege and you'll earn hillwalkers a bad name. So stick to this code of conduct:

■ **Do** the housework: leave the bothy clean, with the fire out and the door firmly shut to keep out animals, and carry out your rubbish (plus any that's been left by visitors with shab-bier consciences).

■ **Don't** presume you have the right to be there: most bothies are privately owned and use is at the discretion of the landowner.

■ **Do** extend your etiquette to the land around the bothy: bury number twos at least 300m/yd away.

■ **Don't** assume you'll be the only people using the bothy: any more than five in your party constitutes an unwelcome crowd.

■ **Do** recognize that fuel is valuable: don't cut live wood, and always leave a supply of dry kindling for the next resident.

■ **Don't** outstay your welcome: use a bothy for a few days at most.

■ **Do** say thanks if you're a regular bothy sleeper: make a donation towards their up-keep. See page 142 for contact details.

Camping and backpacking

Choosing a tent

For sitting out storms and lounging around you need a decent-sized tent, but if you want to backpack, weight is a consideration too.

Choosing the right tent is far from easy. One weekend you may be backpacking, the next you may take a short walk to a wild camp site, and the next you might want to camp from the back of your car. All these uses require different sizes and weights of tent, so deciding what to buy is a tough call.

The key features for such a wide range of uses are living space and weight. For comfort in all weathers your tent needs a large porch to store wet gear and lots of living space to make long stays under the stars comfortable. But if you intend carrying the tent for any length of time, the lighter the better – even if some space is sacrificed.

Fabrics

The big choice is between nylon and polyester. Experts used to say that when new, nylon was stronger and slightly more elastic than polyester, but that polyester was less sensitive to the harmful effects of UV, so it should last longer. However, more recent tests have shown that nylon is in fact less sensitive to UV than polyester, so nylon should last longer. Clearly no one is sure. Polyurethane (PU) is applied to make the fabrics waterproof. The level of waterproofness is indicated by a 'hydrostatic head' rating. So a fabric with a hydrostatic head rating of 10,000mm is more waterproof (and probably more expensive) than a fabric that has a hydrostatic head rating of only 5,000mm. However it has to be said that differing methods of testing mean that these figures should not be taken too literally.

Inner or outer pitched first?

Inner-first pitching saves weight and tends to be stable as the inner and outer contribute to stability. It should be more water-resistant too as there are less complicated sleeves on the flysheet to seal. But when pitched in wet conditions outer-pitched-first designs are better as you can put the outer up, get inside, strip off your wet gear and then put up the inner in the dry. Then, when striking (taking down) the tent you can do the reverse, pack the inner away and get your waterproofs on before hauling down the outer in the rain and packing it away.

Poles

Poles are used to give the tent shape and stability. Most tents have alloy poles with shock-cords down the middle that allow them to be easily folded and opened. Better tents have colour-coded poles so you know which pole goes in which part of the tent. For the greatest stability, look for geodesic designs where the poles cross one another at two or more places. Glass-fibre poles will snap more easily than alloy, particularly in cold weather.

Guylines

A set of cords is usually provided to help hold the tent stable in high winds. Some tent designs need fewer guylines than others, as stability can also be controlled by careful use of the poles.

Pegs

Most tents come with fairly lightweight basic wire skewer-type designs which are fine for general use. But more durable pegs are available for different types of terrain and these can be purchased separately if needed. Some pegs dig painfully into the hands when pushed into the ground so you may want to replace them with more 'hand-friendly' pegs.

Groundsheet

The groundsheet is the part you lie on inside the inner tent. In modern tents it is usually sewn in and seam-sealed to prevent it from leaking.

Porch

This is the large area that's outside the inner tent yet still under the cover of the flysheet. It is ideal for storing wet gear as well as acting as a kitchen in wet weather.

Weight

The lighter the tent, the easier it will be to carry. But the pay-off will usually be a smaller internal space, or a higher price, or both. So choosing a tent is a compromise and only you can decide which model best suits your needs. Solo backpacking tents can weigh as little as 1,300g (2.9lb) to 2,500g (5.5lb). Some are little bigger than a sleeping bag, others could even take two people at a push for one night in an adventure race.

Headroom

In some tents you can only sit up at the highest point, which is usually near the porch and entrance. To be sure you can sit up inside the tent, get a friend to measure your height when sitting and then compare this to the maximum internal height in the specification.

Flysheet

This forms the outside of the tent, and as its job is to keep the rain away from the inner tent it has to be waterproof. A PU (polyurethane) coating is usually applied to the fabric to achieve this. On more expensive tents a coating of silicone elastomer may be applied; this is more durable and more water-repellent than PU.

Mesh netting

Mesh netting on the inner tent reduces weight and packed size, and increases airflow through the tent, which will aid the control of condensation. However, tents with too much mesh netting are colder at night and so are really only suitable for mild weather. The mesh must be fine enough to prevent insects getting in.

Inner tent

You sleep inside the inner tent, so it needs to be dry and spacious. To ensure you do stay dry, the inner must allow warm air to escape to the underside of the flysheet where it may form condensation. There must also be a gap between the inner and the flysheet, so that any condensation on the underside of the flysheet doesn't soak into the inner tent. A better quality inner tent may have a light fluorocarbon finish to repel condensation that falls on to it from the underside of the flysheet. Single-skin tents do not have a separate inner, so the weight savings can be considerable; but the occupants run the risk of coming into contact with the inside of the flysheet where condensation will always collect – which means they could become damp inside the tent. Single-skin tents are generally colder, too.

Doors

The external doors allow entry to the porch and the inner tent. But they also provide ventilation and act as a windbreak and canopy when cooking. Ideally, all zips should have double pullers so that the top or bottom of the door can be opened. Finally it is worth checking that the doors can be rolled back neatly and secured firmly without any fabric dangling into the porch or inner tent.

Sleeping bags

Choosing the right sleeping bag is a crucial part of comfortable camping. And it very much depends on the circumstances you want to use it in. In most situations, a three-season bag will do the job. These are designed for use in spring, summer and autumn at low levels. For wild camping or camping at altitude or in winter, then you may need a four-season bag. The most expensive, lightweight and compact bags use high quality down. Synthetic fillings give cheaper but heavier and more bulky bags. The best synthetic filling is Polarguard, closely followed by Polarsoft and Primaloft.

If you want to save weight when backpacking, choose a three-season down bag. These are not cheap, so it's best to get one that's suitable for a wide temperature range. A comfort temperature rating of –5°C (23°F) should mean the bag is warm enough for most days in a maritime climate. In summer you'll have to open the side zips to remain comfy, while on colder nights simply slip into your base layers before getting into the bag and you'll keep cosy all night.

When it comes to sleeping out in winter, only the best will do. Your sleeping bag needs to keep you warm and comfortable, but still be light and compact enough to carry any distance.

Despite huge technical advances, the most efficient insulation is still a natural product – the down from a goose. As down is so efficient you don't need much of it to keep you warm, so a down bag will be compact and low in weight, meaning you can easily stow a four-season bag in a backpack.

Weight

It's also worth noting that box construction methods produce a lighter bag than other, more elaborate designs; but other methods hold the down in place better for a more even distribution of insulation.

Fill weight

The better the down, in terms of fill power, the less of it you will need to stay warm – so a lower fill weight is required if the best down is used. By comparing the fill weight of bags with identical fill power, you can judge how warm they will be. But construction methods will also affect warmth, particularly over a period of time.

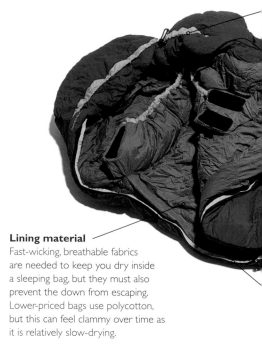

Lining material

Fast-wicking, breathable fabrics are needed to keep you dry inside a sleeping bag, but they must also prevent the down from escaping. Lower-priced bags use polycotton, but this can feel clammy over time as it is relatively slow-drying.

Fill power

This gives a gauge of how efficient the down is at trapping air (and therefore keeping you warm). The higher the number, the better – and a fill power of 750 is the best generally available. However, different test methods can be used to determine fill power, so a 750 fill power down-tested in Europe may rate as 800 or 900 when tested in the US, for exactly the same product.

Temperature ratings

These are only useful as a guide: how warm you feel inside a sleeping bag depends not just on the bag itself but also on your gender, metabolic rate, food intake, exertion levels and environmental conditions such as wind and humidity. Ratings also assume a sleeping mat is used. Manufacturers' claimed ratings can be indicated in various ways. A season rating may be provided, such as three-season, on cheaper bags. Better bags come with a comfort temperature rating and an extreme (low) temperature rating.

Shoulder baffle

Sleeping bags work by trapping air next to the body, and a shoulder or neck baffle helps to keep that warm air inside the bag.

Filling

Eider duck down is the best, but it's also the most expensive, because it has to be hand-picked from the nests as eider ducks are a protected species. Goose down is almost as good, while duck down is a cheaper alternative. The amount of feathers that are mixed with the down affects performance, because feathers don't provide as much insulation as down. The quality of a down is therefore given in terms of how much down and feathers it contains. The best possible down is 96/4 (96 per cent down, 4 per cent feathers) but the feathers have to be removed by hand to achieve this ratio. So usually a 90/10 mixture is used on the best bags, with 70/30 being common on lower-priced bags. Quite simply, the better the down, the more expensive, but also the more efficient it will be – so you'll need less to stay warm.

Shell material

The shell has to breathe to allow condensation out, and yet the holes must be small enough to keep the down trapped inside. Ideally it should also be water-resistant, as down is a poor insulator once wet, so the latest bags use a highly water-resistant shell to combat the damp environment of a tent in winter.

Side zip

Side zips that extend the whole length of the bag are provided so you can get into your bag easily and have a degree of temperature control. Two-way zips are often used so that you can open them at the bottom to allow your feet to cool down. Half-length side zips make a bag lighter and less expensive, but this may render the bag too hot to use in mild weather. The side zip should always have a substantial baffle to prevent draughts and cold spots, while an anti-snag design is essential to prevent the zip from jamming when operated.

Size

The measurements are taken across the largest 'footprint' made by the bag, with a measurement at the shoulders as well as from the head to toe.

Construction

The long-term performance of a sleeping bag is dictated by the construction method used. Basically, the better the construction method, the less opportunity there is for the down to 'migrate' and leave cold spots. A system of fabric baffles inside the bag is designed to trap the down where it is most needed, and the best bags use a number of construction methods to optimize long-term performance.

Sleeping mats

A sleeping mat can greatly improve the quality of a night spent outdoors. They come in a variety of styles from the classic 'karrimat', through to the modern self-inflating mattresses. As usual, which type you choose will depend on your budget and where you intend to use it.

Slip-sliding away?

The main complaint about open-cell self-inflating mats is that the covers tend to be quite slippy, and you can end the night in a huddle in the corner of the tent. Surface treatments are applied to improve the grip between mat, sleeping bag and tent groundsheet, but they are still nowhere near as 'sticky' as closed-cell foam mats, which tend not to suffer from this problem at all.

Comfort

A sleeping mat provides cushioning on hard or rocky ground, so the thicker and to some extent the stiffer the mat, the more comfy it will be. Mats come in a range of thicknesses but of course the thicker the mat, the heavier, the more bulky and the more expensive it will be. Low-priced closed-cell foam mats may compress over time, while better quality ones, along with open-cell mats, tend not to lose their thickness.

Insulation

The problem with a sleeping bag is that the bit beneath your body has all the air squashed out of it. So for extra insulation against the ground, you need to trap air under your body – and a sleeping mat does this, in one of two ways. Closed-cell foam may be used, which traps air pockets within the structure of the material. Alternatively, open-cell foam is used and a covering around the foam traps air. These types of mat have an air valve that allows them to be inflated, and as the foam tends to suck in air once it is unrolled, these are generally described as 'self-inflating' mats. In truth they usually need a puff or two of air to reach full inflation.

The thickness of any mat affects the amount of air it can trap, so you will find that the thicker the mat, the warmer it will be.

Packed size and weight

The lightest mats use closed-cell foam, but these are also the most bulky. Conversely, self-inflating open-cell mats are quite heavy but a little less bulky. So it all depends on how comfy you want to be, and how much weight and bulk you're prepared to carry.

Durability

Self-inflating open-cell foam mats tend to be slightly less durable than closed-cell ones as it is possible to puncture their outer cover. But this is only likely if you use the mat in the open on a prickly surface. Anyway, if punctured the mat is easy to repair with a patch. By contrast, closed-cell foam mats are virtually indestructible and even do their job with chunks torn out of them. Cheaper closed-cell foam mats tend to be less durable than higher-priced models.

Stoves

From the cheap and cheerful Gaz stove to the sophisticated ultralight, you'll want a stove that you can rely on when the day is done and you need a brew. Before you buy one, decide what fuel you want your stove to burn: gas stoves burn pressurized canisters of propane-butane mixes; petrol/automotive gas stoves burn liquid fuels, such as refined petroleum or paraffin; Trangia stoves burn methylated spirits (denatured alcohol). Each has advantages and disadvantages:

Gas

Pros:	Cons:
Gas stoves are easier to use as the canisters are sealed, so there's no messy fuel leaks. They are very light, cheap and packable, and require no priming – great for shorter trips.	They diminish in power as canister pressure drops and are very susceptible to windy conditions. Empty canisters must be carried off the hill and disposed of responsibly.

Multi-fuel

Pros:	Cons:
Some stoves burn petrol and gas – great for travel, when you don't know what fuel you'll be able to buy.	In general, these are heavy and are not as efficient as single-fuel stoves.

Petrol

Pros:	Cons:
Petrol stoves maintain their performance as fuel levels decrease, so with repeated use, they're more powerful than gas stoves. If you are going on a long backpacking trip, fuel consumption is more economical.	Generally speaking, petrol stoves are heavier and require more maintenance than other types. They need 'priming' (pre-heating the element) before using, and must be pumped regularly to maintain fuel pressure. Some petrol stoves do not allow the flame to be lowered for simmering.

Fuel decoder

Fuel names vary considerably around the world, but here are some of the more common equivalents.

Methylated spirits (meths) = Alcohol (USA); Alcool à brûler (France)

Petrol = Automotive gas (USA); benzin (Denmark, Holland, Switzerland, Italy); essence (France). You can use unleaded petrol, or refined petrol such as Coleman fuel (white gas in the USA)

Paraffin = Kerosene (Italy, USA, Australia, Spain); petroleum (Holland, Belgium, Denmark); petrol (Germany, Holland); petrole (France)

Meths

Pros:	Cons:
Meths stoves can never go wrong; there are no mechanical parts. They're much cheaper to run and work well in the wind.	They're not as powerful and are bulky to carry. Refilling while you're cooking can be tricky.

Hillwalking in Winter

Get into the hills in wind and rain, fog and burning sun – you have the kit and the skills. Put a thin veneer of ice down, or clothe the mountains in a blanket of crisp snow and you've stepped up a level. You'll need a few new pieces of kit – at least an ice axe and crampons – and a whole range of new skills to ensure your hillwalking remains safe whilst letting you appreciate the majesty of the mountains in their purest form.

Great hills for beginners

For your first winter walk, try a popular hill that you've already walked in summer, so you'll have some idea of the terrain. Ideally try your first walks in good winter weather with snow on the ground and blue skies overhead. Do remember that it only takes one cloud to roll in over the summit and you will soon be challenging your navigation skills! Clear skies bring low temperatures, which mean the snow and ice will be hard as concrete, so crampons skills will also be very important, particularly on exposed plateaus where the soft snow has been blown clear to expose solid ice.

The easier routes in winter will be those that follow gentle ridges, so you should look for routes that follow ridges with widely spaced contour lines on the map.

What to wear

The first obvious difference between summer and winter walking is the temperatures that you'll be operating in. Dressing correctly for the hills requires a good layering system (see page 26).

Base layers Don't wear cotton next to your skin. Wear a wicking base layer that will move sweat away from your body, keeping you dry and allowing your breathable jacket to work properly.

Mid-layer Again you need a breathable fabric and most people opt for a polyester fleece.

Outer layer As your final layer you need a winter jacket.

Hat You lose most body heat through your head so always take a hat. A Lowe Alpine mountain cap is an excellent option.

Gloves You have a choice of gloves or mitts. Some gloves have linings that can be worn separately, allowing you more dexterity when you need to, for example, use a compass.

Legs Remember to take a pair of waterproof trousers. Gaiters are also useful for keeping snow out of your boots.

What to take

Make sure you pack the following when heading into the hills in winter…

Whistle – six blasts on a whistle at one minute intervals is the standard call in an emergency.

Extra pair of gloves – someone in your party might forget theirs, you might lose yours, or your first pair might get soaked.

Map – everyone in your party should carry a map and compass. A **compass** on a lanyard can be attached to the zip of your map pocket for safekeeping.

First aid kit – you should pack one of these at all times of the year.

Mobile phone – don't rely on one of these as reception in the hills can be poor. But they are useful as a backup and have saved lives.

Sunglasses – eye protection is vital to combat reflected UV rays and wind-blown snow.

Flask – tea and coffee are diuretics (they make you wee) so they aren't good for rehydrating. Instead, try a warm blackcurrant squash, which will help to replace lost energy and keep you hydrated.

Headlamp – most accidents happen in descent when people are tired, hurrying to get down at the end of the day in poor light.

GPS – can be useful but this is not a substitute for a map, compass and sound navigation skills.

Extra food – winter walking requires more energy than summer walking so pack more food in your lunchbox and take an extra supply for emergencies.

An extra warm layer – take a duvet jacket or an extra fleece.

Shelter – a large orange survival bag or a group shelter are essential items.

Boots, crampons and ice axe

If you've never ventured out on to winter hills before, the first thing you're going to need to do is invest in three important bits of gear – an ice axe, a pair of crampons and a pair of winter boots.

Four-season boots

When the snow covers the mountains for days on end it becomes compact and icy, and your average three-season hillwalking boot will crumple into submission when asked to kick a series of steps up a snowy slope in staircase fashion. So for this type of terrain you need dedicated footwear that's stiff enough in the upper and sole to be kicked into a snow slope or worn with crampons all day without allowing the straps to cut into your feet. They call them four-season boots in the outdoor indus-try, but they are really best described as 'fourth season' boots, as they are generally too stiff for comfortable walking below the snowline.

Crampon compatibility

Winter boots have to be compatible with crampons – metal spikes that can be strapped to the outside of the boot for use when walking across frozen ice or snow.

Crampons are graded for stiffness with the letters C1, C2, and C3, and boots are graded for stiffness as B1, B2 and B3. Buy yourself a B1 boot (usually a three–four season boot) and it can only be used with a C1 crampon. Most four-season boots are graded B2 and can be used with a flexible C1 or a less flexible C2 crampon. Ice-climbing boots are totally stiff and graded B3 – these can be used with any crampons.

Ice axes

For simple winter walking a basic axe is fine, being cheaper and often lighter than the stronger mountaineering, or 'technical' axe. Look for a 'T' or a 'B' symbol somewhere on the axe – 'T' is for 'technical' and 'B' is for 'basic'. A technical axe will have a stronger shaft, can be used for belaying and, usually, sports a higher price tag.

Spike

A conical spike on the end of the shaft is better for driving into the ground for stability on steep slopes, whereas a spade-shaped spike is better for self arrest – but there's not enough in it to greatly influence your final choice of axe.

Feel

You want an axe that's light enough to be convenient yet balanced enough to swing efficiently. To test this, swing the axe as if cutting a step, then suddenly stop the movement to see how far your hand is pulled by the momentum. If the axe stops immediately and doesn't pull your hand through, it's probably too light. If your hand is pulled a long way, it may be too heavy or unbalanced: check you are comfortable with the overall weight. Try a few and you'll get a feel for what's going to suit.

Shaft

The length of the shaft is critical: too long and you'll have difficulty swinging it efficiently; too short, and you will have to crouch for support on a slope. Lengths vary from around 50cm (20in) for climbing axes to 90cm (36in) for the longest of walking axes. To find the right size for you, hold the head with your arm by your side – the spike should be about 8cm (3in) from the ground. It also makes it heavier and more expensive. Recently, curved shafts have appeared that make it easier to plunge the shaft into a steep snow slope – and this shape is also better for carrying the axe between your 'sack and back.

Grip

Some ice axes have a means of improving the grip on the shaft. A rubber sleeve or moulding is often used, but these make the axe heavier – and more expensive. However, a rubber grip is far more comfortable, secure and warm than a plain shaft when hacking steps or climbing.

Loops and leashes

Some ice axes are not fitted with a loop or leash. This isn't necessarily a problem, but if you drop the axe, it may skid down the mountain. There are advantages to having an axe without a loop or leash as you are then free to change hands on different terrain. Most people tend to favour the wrist loop as a good general purpose method of staying in contact with their ice axe. Others use a long leash comprising a webbing strap that is attached to the body, rucksack or waistbelt as well as the head of the ice axe. This allows you to change hands more easily on steep slopes.

Pick

The business end of the axe has to be aggressive enough for efficient placement, yet not so steeply angled as to tear itself from your hands when used for ice-axe arrest. Axes with more teeth and a positive point will bite more firmly (better for mountaineers), but for walking the teeth aren't so important. Remember that a point which tapers from the sides will bite less aggressively, leading to a smoother, safer arrest.

Adze

The flat, spade-like area of the head is the adze, and its main use is clearing out snow or ice when cutting steps or building snow holes or other icy constructions. A gentle curve of the adze allows a full arm swing to be used when cutting steps, while a wide adze will clear more snow than a narrow one will.

Crampons

These are for walking across hard snow and ice, and the most important thing is making sure they fit the flex and shape of your boot. If you already have a pair of four-season boots, take them into the shop with you and get the staff to recommend the right crampons. If your boots will take step-in crampons (ones with a heel clip coupled with a single strap and toe cradle) then buy these as they are much easier to fit, especially when you're on a cold hillside.

Fit

It's vital that any crampons you buy fit your boots, so take them with you when you go shopping for crampons (some boots simply don't take some crampons). There is a convenient grading system to help match boots to crampons, so find out whether your boots are B1, B2 or B3 (any shop assistant should be able to tell you) and buy crampons C1, C2 or C3 to match, where 1 is the most flexible and 3 is the stiffest. A stiff B3 boot will take all crampons, but a B1 boot will only take C1 crampons. If you just plan on winter walking, B1 boots and C1 crampons are fine. And bear in mind that crampons may outlast your boots, so look for ones that are highly adjustable. Make sure the crampons are adjusted to fit your boots before setting off on a route, and practise fitting at home as it's much harder with cold fingers on the hill.

Anti-balling plates

To prevent snow from collecting under crampons, anti-balling plates can be fitted to the base. I recommend you use these rubber or plastic accessories, which are provided with some crampons.

Sharpness of points

Some crampons come with extremely sharp spikes which simply mean shredded gaiters and more potentially lethal stumbles – it's much easier to catch them on your inside leg. Sharp points get blunt pretty quickly anyway, so initial sharpness isn't really too important.

Instructions

It's amazing how many crampons still come without instructions, so check in the box to see if your pair has them. If not, ask the shop staff for detailed fitting advice, particularly if you have small boots as you may need to cut off some of the adjuster bar with a hacksaw.

Binding

You'll probably be fitting crampons in pretty foul weather, so choose the easiest strapping system that the design of your boots will allow. Binding systems come in two types – step-in and strap-on. Step-in crampons are much quicker to fit but require stiffer boots and are usually rated C2 and C3. They have a heel clip coupled with a single strap to a toe bail (the plastic, metal or nylon frame that fits over the toe of the boot). Strap-on crampons, although a little more fiddly, fit a wider variety of boots. To see how easy your crampons are to fit, borrow a thick pair of gloves from the gear shop and wear them while you attach the crampons to your boots you'll get a good idea of how fiddly they are going to be to fit on the hill.

Points

In general, walker's crampons have ten downward-pointing spikes. Crampons with 12 or 14 points may have forward-facing points for tackling steeper snow slopes. You may not need them every day, but they can be useful once you start more regular winter walking on steeper ground. Longer points will give you a firmer grip in deep and soft snow, but they may also mean that you'll trip over more easily, so shorter spikes are more suitable for first-time users.

Route planning

Navigating becomes a great deal harder in winter conditions. Even something as simple as taking a compass bearing can leave your fingers numb, and matters get a great deal harder when you're in white-out conditions. Trying to keep a map still on a summit in high winds or grappling with a compass in the bitter cold are not easy things to do.

But quite a lot of the problems with winter navigation can be overcome with careful route planning before you even get out on to the hill.

1 Plan your route and note down all important bearings (such as the one needed to get off the summit) on a sheet of paper that you can leave in your map case.

2 Work out pacing distances between features before you go. If you're coming off a summit and need to find a turn for a path that is 100m/yd away, it's much easier if you've worked out the bearing and know roughly how many paces to take to get there.

3 Make a note of features that you will be looking to 'tick off' on each section of the route. A lake, wall or ridge are all good. You will need to look carefully to spot certain features in snow – a frozen lake will appear as a flat area, a cairn as a smooth, snow-covered lump and a path as a slight indentation.

4 Choose a route that avoids cliffs and narrow ridges because these will be more difficult in snowy conditions, as they will be draped in cornices (snow that projects a few metres over the edge of the cliff) and it's easy to step over them in a white-out. Deep snow gathers in hollows and lee slopes, while easier terrain will be found on broad ridges and windward slopes.

5 Make a note of any escape routes in case conditions become too tricky. The worst weather

will be on the summit, so look out for any shelter on the way up and use it to check your position, set your compass or simply think without the elements battering you senseless. Any time visibility is bad, you need greater accuracy in your navigation. The best way of measuring distance is by dividing the route into small sections or routes – say, less than 300m/yd – and counting your paces. You can do this by having plenty of identifiable features on your route.

Safety tip

When hillwalking in winter, safety is of primary importance. Let someone know where you are going, what your route will be and when you intend to be back. And once you're back, let them know you're safe.

Your kit

Keep your map in a map case and stow it inside your jacket chest pocket with the cord attached to a zip puller or equivalent. Always keep a spare map in your rucksack. Store your compass in a chest pocket with the cord attached to a zip puller.

Using an ice axe

An ice axe, after a stiff-soled pair of boots, is your most important winter tool. It can provide support and balance when you're walking on steep terrain and it allows you to cut steps on short sections of hard snow. The most vital function of an ice axe is to prevent you from sliding down the side of a mountain, if you slip up. This is one of the most common accidents in the winter hills, so knowing how to use your axe could save your life.

In the next few pages you'll find everything you need to know about ice axe technique, from cutting simple steps to stopping a potentially fatal, head-first slide on your back.

Carrying an ice axe

Dedicated ice axe attachments on the back of your rucksack are good for transporting the axe to and from the hills. Unfortunately, they don't offer easy access once on the mountain, particularly if you need it in a hurry. Alternatives include using the compression straps on the side of the sack (make sure the pick faces backwards) or using the shoulder strap.

The easiest way of storing an axe on a walk where you will need it regularly but not all the time, is to carry it on your back. To place it, simply take hold of your rucksack strap, push the axe through and slide behind the shoulder. Remember to remove the axe before you take your rucksack off or you will lose it.

You can, of course, just carry your axe in your hand. This allows you to use it in an instant. The correct hold is with the pick facing backwards and the adze facing forwards, with thumb and forefinger around the front. The middle finger runs down the shaft and the other two fingers curl around the pick. This ensures the axe can be moved into arrest position as quickly as possible. Always carry it in the 'uphill' hand.

Where to practise

Start by finding a good slope – it should be concave with a safe run-out (in case you fail to arrest), with no rocks, trees or people to crash into. It will need to be steep enough to slide on, but this largely depends on snow conditions (you will go faster on hard snow than on soft). Also be aware of possible dangers from above – rock falls from cliffs or climbers, or other walkers who might drop ice or equipment. Wear a helmet at all times.

Cutting steps

If you haven't got crampons or you need to cross just a short stretch of snow, cutting a series of steps in the snow will allow you to negotiate a short icy section with minimal hassle. When cutting steps it is vital that they run parallel to the slope (ie left to right) and are flat, so you'll have to be aware of the natural tendency to cut slightly uphill (your feet will simply slide down and out of the step). To guard against this, make sure your shoulders are at right angles to the slope and the step you cut will be parallel to the slope. The other thing to remember is to cut your steps so they tilt into the slope – this will make the steps positive and make using them much easier.

1 Kick or chop a couple of steps on the practice slope (to stop you from slipping) and then turn your body sideways to the incline. Hold the axe in your uphill hand, with the adze pointing backwards. Now swing the arm in an arc to begin cutting the step. Remember, this is not a test of strength. Five or six controlled slashes are better than a single, almighty punt – it's important that you keep your balance.

Ice axe arresting

The most common cause of accidents is a slip on steep ground and not being able to stop, but your best defence is not the ice axe – it's a pair of stiff-soled boots. Not falling over in the first place is the real key, but if you do slip, there are ways of stopping. You need to practise the techniques, on your left- and right-hand sides, until they become second nature.

2 Once you have cut a suitable foothold, step into it and cut your next step. Remember to keep your body at right angles to the slope and to keep your axe swings steady. As you progress you will notice that you are climbing diagonally, so at some point you are going to need to turn around.

3 When you decide you want to turn, cut one more step, big enough for both feet. Then take hold of the axe head (with the pick facing out the back of the hand), step into the ledge and plunge the axe spike into the snow for stability.

4 With both hands on the axe, turn your feet until they face the other way. Swivel the axe in its hole as you change hands, ensuring the pick points out of the back of the new (uphill) hand.

5 You are now ready to continue up or down the slope. Turn the axe around, making sure that the adze is facing backwards. Ensure that you are standing with your body side-on to the slope and start to cut steps.

The arrest position

The correct position is with one hand on the axe head, pick facing forwards, and the other hand on the point at the bottom to stop it digging into the snow or your body. The adze should sit tucked into the shoulder, in the hollow beneath the collarbone, and the shaft should cross the body at roughly 60 degrees.

The basic ice axe arrest

This is the most fundamental and easiest of all types of ice axe arrest. It assumes you are sliding down the hill on your back.

1 Slide down the slope a few times to get familiar with the movement, but don't carry an axe. Then do it a few times with the axe in your hand. Make sure you aren't wearing crampons when you're practising, or you run the risk of serious injury.

4 Bringing your full bodyweight over the axe will quickly arrest your slide. You can also plough your helmet into the snow to stop more quickly, but expect a face full of snow!

Head-first arrest

If you find yourself sliding head first then you'll need to turn yourself around before you begin to arrest your slide. To practise this technique, cut a bucket seat in the snow to hook your feet into, or get a friend to hold your legs, while you lie on your front, with your head facing down the slope.

2 Stand somewhere you aren't likely to slide and practise moving the axe into the arrest position (see box left). Make sure you practise this on both sides, holding the head of the axe correctly in both right and left hand. When you're confident doing that standing up, slide down the slope again and practise bringing the axe into the arrest position across your chest.

3 Now you're ready to start the actual ice axe arrest. Slide down the hill and bring the axe into the ice axe arrest position. Now roll over on to the axe, making sure you roll towards the side of the pick (ie if it's tucked into your right shoulder, roll right, and vice versa). Then lean all your weight over the axe, being sure to face away from the adze to avoid injury if the axe hits a shallow rock and bounces back. It is vital to keep your feet raised into the air here because when you need to do this for real, you might be wearing crampons.

1 **The turn** As you begin to slide, grasp the axe as you would with any arrest – with one hand on the head, the other on the spike – and reach out as far as you can, on the side you're holding the pick. Make sure you don't plunge the head in as the resistance could rip it out of your hands. Instead angle the pick so it faces up-slope, then press down (see 'Angling the pick', page 116).

2 With the axe pick digging into the snow, you will begin to turn around. Keep your knees in the air and when your body is half way around, remove the pick and you will continue to rotate.

3 **The arrest** Because you cannot brake effectively with the axe at arm's length, as it will be after turning from the head-first arrest, you will need to perform a separate manoeuvre. The first part is to remove the axe, arch your back and assume the standard arrest position (with the adze tucked into your shoulder and the shaft angled across your body).

4 Once you're in this position you can now plunge down to arrest your slide, with the axe held in the strongest position to stop you.

Angling the pick

Because during the early stages of the head-first and upside-down arrests the axe will be at arm's length, you will not have a very strong hold on it. This makes it vital that you angle the pick to prevent it from catching and tearing itself from your hands. To do this, when holding the axe out, be sure to angle the

pick slightly uphill (with the adze angling down) and apply enough pressure to turn. This should ensure the axe doesn't 'bite' and get torn from your hands.

Upside-down arrest

This is the hardest arrest to perform and one well worth practising. Like the head-first arrest, it is divided into two procedures – the turn and the arrest. Start by digging a bucket seat and sitting in it, upside down, or get a friend to hold your feet.

1 **The turn** Holding your axe in the normal way (one hand over point, the other on the head), move it out to the right and press the pick into the snow, tilting it up-slope to ensure it does not 'bite' and get ripped from your hands. You will begin to turn.

2 As you turn you'll need to perform a kind of sit-up manoeuvre to ensure that your feet swing below you, and you end up on your chest rather than your back.

3 **The arrest** This is essentially the same as the arrest stage for the upside-down arrest. Start by arching the back and removing the pick.

Skills

116

3

4

4 With the pick removed, place the axe in the arrest position (adze in shoulder, shaft angled across body) and plunge down to arrest as normal.

Winter boots and crampons

Stopping a fall with your ice axe is one thing, but staying upright in the first place is the most important rule of winter walking. To help you, there are two very important tools – the winter boot and the crampon.

Boots – an essential winter tool

Boots are the most important single tool for the winter walker. They need to be stiff enough to kick steps easily and take crampons, yet comfortable enough to walk in all day. But you

need to know how to use them. Read this section, practise on a safe slope, and you'll be steady for the winter season.

Slice steps

These are among the most commonly used steps and they use the edge of the sole to cut a platform. So, standing parallel to the slope on a pre-cut platform, kick your uphill boot across the slope to cut a step. If you need to, be sure to take a couple of kicks to create a step that is big enough, then step up into it with your uphill foot and bring your lower foot into the step just vacated. Repeat the process as you work your way uphill in what will be a zig-zag fashion.

Take a couple of kicks to make the step.

Use the edge of your sole, not the heel.

Turning

Because you'll be moving diagonally up, at some point you'll need to turn. To do this, cut

Kick a step large enough for two feet.

Turn round and start again.

a longer than usual platform with your uphill foot so it can accommodate both feet. Now step into it and, using your ice axe for support, turn to face the opposite direction. You will now be able to continue cutting steps as before, only your uphill and downhill feet will have swapped around.

Pigeon-hole steps

These are great for ascending steep slopes and they are very simple. Start by facing up the slope and kicking the toes of your boots into the snow using your knee as the pivot (this is less tiring than swinging from the hip). The depth of the step you end up with depends entirely on the consistency of the snow, but if it's too hard then you will have to use crampons (see 'front pointing' on page 120).

Kick from the knee.　　Use the axe for balance.

Expert's tip

Be sure to keep the toe lower than the heel to ensure the step stays 'positive', which means only the front of your boot will be in contact with the snow. You'll also need your ice axe handy for support.

Heel plunge steps

This is an extremely useful and very easy way of descending in snow that is not too hard, although you do have to be wary of sudden patches of névé (very hard snow) or ice. The

technique uses your whole bodyweight to create safe steps.

Start with the axe in your preferred hand and the pick facing backwards. Raise your first foot level with the axe.

As you step forwards and down, plunge your heel into the snow and simultaneously plunge your axe in beside it.

With the axe still in your favourite hand, step your other foot through and repeat the action.

Repeat this process all the way down the slope. It may look silly but it's efficient and safe.

Crampons
Putting on crampons

How you do this depends entirely on the type of crampons used, so follow individual manufacturers' instructions. However, there are some general rules. For a start, life is infinitely easier if you can fit them on a level piece of snow or on a rock and not halfway up a dangerous slope. Also, make sure you knock any excess snow from your boots and crampon lugs (if you have them). Now place the crampons neatly on the ground and step into them. Then, if you have step-ins, fit the toe bail first, then the heel clip and finally thread the strap and tighten. Or, if you have strap-in

angled slopes, there is one golden rule, which is to always make sure that all points have contact with the snow. This means 'flat footing', which is where, because you keep all spikes in contact with the snow, your feet can be pointing down across the slope to an angle of up to 45 degrees (see sequence, below left).

When you need to turn, be sure to face down the slope as it's much more stable to have the whole crampon in contact with the snow than just the front points.

bindings, follow the pattern as recommended by the manufacturer. Be sure to tidy away any stray straps and re-tighten them after a few minutes' use.

Before you attempt any kind of incline, practise on the flat. Walk with an imaginary 'no-go area' around each foot to ensure you don't catch your points on trousers, gaiters or straps – this is sometimes called the 'wet nappy waddle'. When you get on moderately

Crampon tips
All balled up

In warm conditions, either from thaw or sunshine, slushy snow can build on the underside of the crampon and negate the grip afforded by the points. The most effective solution is to buy anti-balling plates, rubber undersoles that shed the snow (bottom right). The other is to regularly tap the snow from your feet with the shaft of your axe as you walk (below).

Adjusting crampons

Because it'll be cold and probably unpleasant to have bare hands for too long on the hills, it's best to fit your crampons to your boots at home. However, if you use more than one pair of boots it's easy to forget, so always carry a tool on to the hill so you can adjust them.

Getting snagged

The greatest cause of accidents with crampons is getting them caught in gaiter buckles or baggy trousers. Make sure your gaiters don't have buckles on the inside, and that any loose straps or cords are tucked out of the way. Similarly, remember to fit each crampon to the correct foot, ensuring the buckle is always on the outside.

Front pointing

This is very similar to using your boots to cut pigeon-hole steps, only with crampons on. It is the main technique for ascending steep slopes and for snow- and ice-climbing. So, just as you kicked steps with your boots, you now kick your front points into the snow or ice, making

sure you keep your foot horizontal. While this may feel insecure at first, with a stiff pair of boots you are in fact remarkably stable. It does tire the calves very quickly, though.

If the incline is not too steep, then a less tiring alternative is the American technique. This is basically a halfway house between front pointing and flat footing, with one foot front pointing and the other placed facing down the slope with all the points in contact with the snow (flat footing).

And finally...

Be careful at the end of your session when your body has grown used to walking with crampons. After removing them it is not unusual to step confidently off across the ice and end up on your bottom.

Camping in winter

Don't be in any doubt how cold the hills can get: the coldest temperature recorded in Britain was −27.2°C (−17°F), in Braemar, Aberdeenshire, in 1982 (and again in Altnaharra, Highland, in 1995). And don't forget that the temperature normally decreases by around 1°C per 150m height rise (5.4°F per 1,000ft) – Braemar is only 339m (1,112ft) above sea-level. In continental Europe and North America temperatures can fall way below this. Make sure your sleeping bag is up to the job by checking its temperature rating (usually written on the label inside the bag). If it's a three-season bag (usually rated as 'comfortable at' around −5°C/23°F) or old, invest in a three—four or four-season bag, or upgrade it with a fleece liner: it'll add an extra 5°C (9°F) for 570g (1.3lb). Check that your sleeping mat is in good condition too – you must effectively insulate yourself from the ground.

Pitch wisely

Choosing a site is a trickier business in winter:

- Avoid pitching in hollows: these tend to fill with cold air.
- Avoid any spots that may funnel wind, such as cols. An 8km/h (5mph) wind can have the same effect as a temperature drop of 2°C (4°F), a 48km/h (30mph) wind is equivalent to a drop of 20°C (36°F) .
- Pay attention to the terrain and consider possible sites in terms of weather changes. If there's a sharp downpour, how likely is that riverbank to flood? Check your map for clues too: what seems like solid ground now could turn into a bog if it thaws overnight. And it sounds obvious but, if snow is lying, ensure you're not in danger of avalanche: avoid camping below cliffs or steep slopes.
- In non-snowy conditions, look for areas below high ground, in the lee of the wind. These are rain shadow areas: the clouds deposit their cargo of rain on the mountain before they reach you. In these areas, under certain weather conditions, a peculiarity known as the föhn effect also occurs as air descends and warms. While it's a more common phenomenon in the Alps, it does happen in Britain and creates warmer areas – up to 16°C (29°F) higher on a few rare occasions.

Pitch on snow

It goes without saying that you must be 100 per cent confident that your chosen spot isn't in avalanche danger. It's worth digging down a few centimetres/inches (especially if the snow is slabby, as you'll quickly be able to clear away blocks of snow) to create a sheltered site. Now stamp all over the site to create a firm layer of snow – both where you'll be pitching your tent and around the entrance to avoid

snow being blown inside. Smooth over to flatten. If you have time, wait for 20 minutes to let the snow harden again. Now pitch your tent, making sure the rear is towards the prevailing wind, to avoid snow building up at the entrance. Use snow stakes to peg out the tent – these bury in the snow sideways, but make sure you pack the snow around them to create a solid anchor.

Hypothermia

Hypothermia is a killer. Don't go winter camping – or even winter hillwalking – without implanting these basic facts in your brain. Hypothermia occurs when your core body temperature drops and your body doesn't have the energy to reverse the decline.

You'll get exposure first – you'll feel cold, shiver and may experience cramp or pins and needles. Hypothermia follows unless you take action to warm your body up – expect uncontrollable shivering, uncoordinated movement, blurred vision and slurred speech. You'll also behave unreasonably and your judgment will be impaired. Untreated, you'll fall unconscious, then into a coma, and will finally die.

What to do

Treat hypothermia as a medical emergency. At the FIRST sign of cold, add layers of clothing, find shelter, eat, have a hot drink and consider whether to use your escape route. If you've ignored the initial signs of cold and developed exposure, do all of the above and go home. Straightaway. If you've developed hypothermia, your mates will have to arrange that on your behalf: they should call mountain rescue, get you inside a sleeping bag and bivy bag, insulated from the ground, and get you to hospital as soon as is humanly possible.

Avalanches

An avalanche occurs when the gravitational pull on the snow is greater than the forces holding it together. Over the winter many layers of snow build up. Each is set down under very different conditions and bonds differently with adjoining layers. Between snowfalls, the temperature may rise. This can melt or expose surface layers which, when they re-freeze, cause a smoother, less stable surface for the next snowfall to bond with. Rain between snowshowers can also cause a slicker surface that weakens the bonds between the layers. Light snowfalls and consistently cold temperatures tend to strengthen the snowpack and make avalanches less likely.

The three main ingredients are:

- **Slope angle** Most avalanches occur on slopes of between 30 and 45 degrees, but they can happen on any slope given the right conditions.
- **Snow cover** Avalanches are most likely to occur either during or immediately after significant snowfall. The 24 hours following a snowfall is the most critical period.
- **Temperature changes** Warm temperatures lasting a couple of days cause melting within the snowpack. This can weaken the bonds between layers of snow and increases the avalanche risk.

Types of avalanche

An avalanche can occur when one layer of snow slides over another (known as a surface avalanche) or when the whole snow cover slides over the ground (a full-depth avalanche). An avalanche may be dry or wet according to whether free water is present in the snow. It may be of loose snow (when the snow starts at a single point) or a slab avalanche (which occurs when an area of more cohesive snow separates from the surrounding pack and slides out).

Avoiding avalanche-prone areas

Avalanche risk can be avoided by careful route choice. Think about the following factors:
- **Slope** Most large slab avalanches run on slopes between 30 and 45 degrees.
- **Ground surface** Smooth ground such as rock slab is more likely to experience a full-depth avalanche. Rough ground with large boulders will anchor the snow better, but once these rocks are covered there is an equal risk of a surface avalanche occurring.
- **Slope profile** Convex (bulging) slopes are more likely to avalanche and the point where the angle of convexity is greatest is where a slab avalanche is most likely to start (see below).

- **Ridges** The crests of main ridges are usually protected from avalanche but keep clear of areas where a cornice (a build-up of snow overhanging the mountain) may have accumulated.
- **Lee slopes** Here snow tends to build up quite deeply and there can be a particular risk following a heavy snowfall. Wind tends to deposit snow in sheltered areas. So if there is a south-west wind of 40km/h (25mph) with freezing temperatures indicated, then there will be an avalanche hazard on north-east slopes.
- **Vegetation** A slope with plenty of vegetation can help the snow 'stick' to the mountain and may also block the path of an avalanche. But, conversely, single trees may cause a fracture line in the snow that can increase the avalanche risk.

Test for an avalanche

Part of becoming avalanche-savvy is being able to assess the risk on a particular slope. The first thing to do is to be aware of the predicted likelihood of an avalanche (get an avalanche forecast if one is available) and be aware of what the weather has been doing over the last few days (has there been a snow-fall in the last 24 hours, or a period of much warmer weather?).

Using your eyes is also a good way of assessing risk. Can you see any evidence of avalanche as you walk towards the hill? Where is the snow tending to accumulate? Note areas of cornice build-up above you and see how the snow is behaving as you walk on it. Is it coming away in small slabs under foot?

To gauge the risk of a particular slope, dig a snowpit on a small, safe slope with a similar aspect and angle to the hill you want to assess.

1 Isolate a block with a back wall that is roughly waist deep. (See pictures below.)

2 Brush off the back wall and look for different layers of snow. You need to assess layers on how hard they are and how wet they are. Can you push your whole fist, all your fingers, or just a single finger into the layer? Then look at how wet it is – can you form a snowball? Can you squeeze water out of it? Is it just slush? If there is a big difference between how hard and wet layers are, then there is an increased risk of avalanche. It's a good idea to slice a compass or an old credit card down through the snow, as this is a very good way of spotting different layers that are hard to detect.

3 Try the wedge block test. Insert your ice axe at the back of the block, and give it a steady pull towards you. If any part of the block easily separates from the snow, the avalanche risk is high. If you spend a lot of time in the hills in winter it's worth getting on a course to hone your avalanche awareness.

Appreciating the hills

Being in the hills means coming across breath-taking views, entertaining incidents and the need to prove that you really did make it to the summit. It is therefore very likely that you will want to record your trips in photographic form to keep sharp your memories of great days out. The photography section here gives you a few basic tips to help you get the most from your camera amongst the crags.

An adage made popular in the 1930s ran thus: 'Take nothing but photographs, leave nothing but footprints' – the final section looks at the environmental harm caused by hillwalking and suggests a handful of ways you can lessen the impact.

If you need to know more when planning a trip, or are thinking about booking a training course, check the useful addresses at the end for further information.

■ Photography

Everyone can take decent mountain photos — all you need is a camera, film (or memory card) and a bit of know-how. He are some tips from professional photographers.

Books and magazines are packed with stunning mountain pictures, thanks to their teams of expert photographers. They know that there's an art to taking great pictures of people outdoors, and a lot of their techniques

Camera bags — These come from a variety of manufacturers such as Camera Care Systems, Tamrac or Lowepro. Pouches are worn on a waist belt. They're great for getting the camera out in a hurry and they keep your hands free for scrambling.

Tripod — Useful for evening pictures when light is low. Small tabletop tripods are very useful as you can raise their height, say by balancing them on a rock.

Filters — These are another way you can take creative control of your pictures. A grey graduated filter, such as a Cokin G1, and a circular polarizer are useful in the hills.

Invest in a **skylight** or **UV filter** to protect your lens and make sure you clean the lens to maintain picture quality and protect gear.

Camera body — A basic, fully manual SLR camera body and standard 50mm lens are very affordable. Invest a bit more and you can buy a camera that has a range of modes (for portraits, low light situations, landscapes, fast action, etc). This takes a lot of the worry out of photography, but it also means you miss out on having creative control of your pictures. Digital SLR bodies are a bit more expensive but you may be able to attach your existing lenses.

Flash — Many SLR cameras come with a built-in flash which is useful for fill-in light in certain situations. You may want to invest in a separate flash gun.

Lenses — The great thing about SLR cameras is that you can change the lens for different situations. For use in the hills keep things simple — just a 20mm (wide-angle) lens, which is great for dynamic close-range portraits and landscapes, and a 100mm (telephoto) lens for scrambling portraits from a distance, which helps to isolate the subject from the background.

aren't dependent on expensive photographic equipment. By following a few of their simple rules anyone can inject a bit of variety and life into their photos.

So even if you've only got a compact camera, here are a few ideas to help you start taking fantastic pictures on your next trip into the hills.

Basic camera gear

You can take great pictures in the hills with a basic compact or point-and-shoot digital camera following these composition tips. But if you want more control over your pictures, using shutter speed, aperture size and creative filters, you'll probably want to use an SLR (single lens reflex) camera. Here's a basic, affordable set-up that will cover any situation in the hills.

Digital SLRs are more expensive, but allow you to email photos and (if you've got the right software) to remedy basic errors when you get back home.

Which film?

If you are shooting conventionally to film, you need to know a little about film speed. The higher a film's ISO number, the more sensitive it is to available light. This means that a 'fast' film (eg ISO 400, ISO 800 or ISO 1600) can be used in low light conditions with less risk of camera shake, as you won't need to make such long exposures as you would with a slow film (such as ISO 50 or ISO 100).

Faster films generally produce grainier, grittier-looking results. This is ideal for some creative effects, especially in black and white, taken on a claggy wet and overcast day. However, often the grain will interfere with the clarity of intricate details and the apparent sharpness of the overall image.

Many professionals use slow Fuji Velvia ISO 50 slide film which is famous for its superb depth of colour, even on the greyest of days. But if light levels are really low they might switch to a faster ISO

This picture was taken using 1600 ISO film. Notice how grainy the picture quality is.

This picture was taken the previous day using fine grain Velvia 50 ISO film, ideal for good light.

speed film such as a 400 or even a 1600 as these films are more sensitive to available light. Black and white film produces some great effects in very 'flat' lighting conditions and when the weather is really moody. On digital cameras you can imitate these effects by using different settings, but ultimately the final results will vary depending on the quality of the camera and how you to choose to view the final images.

Quick tricks to great pictures

Vary camera height

Be prepared to lie down and get your clothes dirty when taking pictures on the hill: varying the height and angle of your camera has to be the quickest and easiest way to inject a fresh perspective into your photos. So, before you take any picture, ask yourself whether it's worth crouching down or standing on raised ground for a more dynamic view, and walk around your subject before you shoot.

Think about foreground interest

If your pictures seem a little boring, it's a good idea to think of the view in terms of three layers: the fore-ground (nearest the camera), the middle ground and the background (off to the horizon). When you're standing on a mountain summit, it's all too easy to point the camera at the distant view without including any foreground. Yet the area that is

Photography

129

the full drama of the scenery. Look for the following:

Bright sunlight. Shafting light through a blanket of storm clouds; you know it's Judgment Day and the sun beams down in brilliant 'Armageddon' rays as though He is casting His fierce and omnipotent fury on the unrepentant souls below… Any peak that is captured in this light will hark back to a scene from the Old Testament. Perfect for a dramatic shot on a biblical scale.

Grey, claggy or misty. With stark rocks and crags looming out at you from low cloud or mist, you're ideally placed for Gothic Horror-style pictures. For best results load up with a fast, grainy black and white film such as ISO 1600 Fuji Neopan. Light levels will be low if the sun is completely blotted out by cloud, so take a mini-tripod along in order to avoid camera shake.

Warm afternoon glow. Late afternoon is the ideal time for

immediately in front of the camera is very useful for providing a sense of depth and scale for the view beyond, helping to bring the viewer into the picture. That's where a person, boulder or cairn comes in handy. For example, the excellent slab on the way up Snowdon adds depth and interest to the picture on the previous page.

warm, honey-coloured mountain pictures as the slopes bask demurely in soft, golden light. As the sun slips towards the horizon, its rays have to penetrate more atmospheric haze (which allows only the shorter, redder rays

Make the most of natural light

The key to perfect hill photos is fantastic weather conditions and interesting light. Both will help reveal the shape of the mountains and convey

to pass) with the result that pictures taken at this time of day are bound to look warmer, more welcoming and more chocolate-boxy. You could sell copies to the local tourist board.

Dawn. Camp out on the hills under canvas, wake up early and (if you're in luck) you'll be rewarded with an unbeliev-able sunrise in every shade of scarlet. When shooting into the sun, you can let the cam-era do all the work. Set to auto exposure it will turn any landscape feature into a stark silhouette against the pink skyline. To make the most of it, try to get down low (or tilt the camera so the horizon lies low in frame) and find a shapely foreground rock or cairn to discover its silhouette potential.

Flat lighting, dull or brood-ing skies. Switch to black and white film in this case. Any mountain scene can be radically transformed by putting a black and white film

in your camera, instead of colour. It's especially useful on grey or overcast days when a scene can be stripped down to its bare essentials to enhance its mood and drama, allowing you to reveal textures and shapes which would be lost in colour. If you're keen on printing your own pictures at home, you'll start here. You can also develop black and white film at many High Street developers and online suppliers.

Use the 'rule of thirds'

This nifty trick has become a bit clichéd, but there's still plenty of mileage in it, as it helps create a more organized and visually pleasing balance in a picture. Basically, imagine a nine-piece grid over the viewfinder (see above), and position any horizontal and vertical elements on the imaginary lines, and any key points of interest within the composition at an intersection of the imaginary lines. See how the model in the picture is on one line and the mountain's summit falls on another.

Lead the eye with a line

Direct attention into the picture area using a lead-in line – any line or curve that directs the eye towards the subject. Good examples might include a path snaking into the frame, a railway line, fence, wall, mountain ridge or river. Just place your subject strategically at the end of the line, and the line will serve to point out the subject and emphasize it.

Zoom in or out

Got a zoom lens or telephoto? Try altering the viewfinder view by zooming in to help isolate the subject better, then zooming back out to see if the subject looks better in its new setting. Telephoto lenses are also very useful for taking portraits of people on the hills. Focus on your subject and the lens will blur the background which helps to simplify what might be a messy backdrop to the picture. The top picture on page 133 was taken using a 20mm wide-angle lens, which has a much bigger depth of field (ie keeps foreground and background in focus better). Thus the mountain in the background (Tryfan in North Wales) is still relatively in focus. Using a longer or telephoto lens would tend to blur the background.

Filter the sky

Graduated filters are handy accessories which take up very little space in your camera bag and are certainly worth their weight. They work by holding back the amount of light reaching the film through the lens, in effect helping you to balance out the contrast between land and sky.

Seven deadly sins

Follow these expert tips to avoid dull hill pics.

1 Two black eyes
When the sun is shining brightly at midday it casts short, harsh shadows. This leads to flat-looking 2D landscapes, washed-out colours and deep black sockets for your subject's eyes. The problem is compounded when the subject is also wearing a peaked cap. The answer is to switch on your camera's flash to help

light up the darker shadow areas, or time your summit push for earlier or later in the day.

Professional's tip
Morning and afternoon offer soft sunlight and longer shadows that help sculpt the scene to reveal the mountains.

2 Wot no sky?
Mountain pictures are frequently spoilt with a bland, white or washed-out sky. This is because film cannot record extremes of contrast between a bright sky and dark foreground and will overexpose the sky as a result. One answer is to slip a filter over the lens such as a grey graduated filter. This will help balance out the contrast and retain some detail in the sky. Another answer is to frame up the shot so there's relatively little or no sky in the composition.

Professional's tip
Graduated filters come in different strengths and colours. Stick to basic grey as others can look garish.

3 Just plain boring
Sometimes a fantastic view just doesn't translate on film. Organize the scene so there's a focal point somewhere in frame that will act as

an anchor: a summit cairn, lonely tree, even a humble sheep will help the picture seem more meaningful and give a sense of depth. Use the rule of thirds to help compose it.

Professional's tip
The rule of thirds will help you compose a picture, but never be a slave to rules.

4 The little people
When you're taking a portrait of your pals on the hill, take a tip from Michael Caine in the film *Zulu*: don't shoot until you can see the whites of their eyes. If you can't see your subjects' facial expressions you're too far away, so either move your feet and walk closer, or use the camera lens to zoom in so they fill the frame nicely. Get some personality and animated expressions in your shots.

Professional's tip
Some of the best portraits are shot at very close range using a 20mm wide-angle lens. Don't be afraid of invading personal space... get in close and snap!

5 Drizzly clag-fest
In general, colour film is better suited to deep blue summer and autumn skies, sunsets, sunrises and warm-toned late afternoon sunshine. On grey and stormy days, black and white really comes into its own, as wilderness, stripped down to monochro-matic shapes and textures, can enhance the mood.

Professional's tip
Other solutions for bad weather include getting in close to people or natural details – crop out the sky wherever possible. Make sure you keep the camera dry!

6 Busy backgrounds
Messy, over-complicated backgrounds will spoil even the most wonderful mountain view. Watch out for litter, rucksacks, plastic carrier bags and even strangers sneaking into frame, as these will all distract attention away from the main subject. Keep the image as simple as possible, with a clear, clean backdrop behind the subject, and remember to check all four corners of the viewfinder before finally committing the picture to film.

Professional's tip
Be patient and polite with strangers on the hill interfering with your composition – they'll move out of the way eventually.

7 Blurry prints
If a number of your prints come back blurred, it could be that you're not holding the camera securely enough. Stand with your feet hip-distance apart and brace your elbows so they're tucked into your body. Squeeze

the shutter button slowly without jarring the camera – or better still, secure it to a mini-tripod resting on a boulder so as to keep the camera steady.

Professional's tip

SLR users find they can handhold the camera at slow shutter speeds such as 1/15sec, by utilizing the motordrive.

Get the perfect summit shot

A large part of taking a great summit portrait comes from getting your subjects to feel re-laxed and confident in front of the camera.

- Keep them talking about something unre-lated, so they don't feel too self-conscious.
- Think about where you want them to pose. Beside or on top of the trig pillar is a good bet, or at the edge of the summit, looking out. If you've got three or more people in frame, try to vary head height so you create a more dynamic shape and use the available space more creatively.

- Whichever pose they strike for the camera, try to make it animated, so they don't look like a row of stuffed armadillos. Good ideas include standing triumphant on the trig pil-lar or lying collapsed at the bottom of it, or tucking into sandwiches while admiring the view and pointing. If they're too knackered by the ascent, wait for them to get their breath back completely, and are feeling good about their achievement, before tackling the portrait.
- Move closer in to get your subject to fill the frame (or use the camera's zoom). And don't forget to turn the camera on its side for a vertical full- or three-quarters-length portrait as well.
- If you want to include the view too, keep the camera horizontal. Be sure to focus on the subject, then (keeping your finger gently on the shutter button to lock focus) reframe the shot so the subject lies just off-centre, looking at the camera or towards the view – into the picture area, not gazing out of it.

Hillwalking and the environment

Your boots are just one pair among the many millions that tramp our paths every year, and every footstep has the potential to cause erosion. But, with a little inside knowledge, you can change the world, one step at a time.

Upland areas may seem pretty tough, but we're gradually becoming more aware of just how fragile they really are. Erosion due to walkers is a small problem compared to overgrazing, acid rain, superquarries, unchecked conifer planting, and global warming. But while our impact is relatively small, the effects are usually concentrated in certain areas. We've all seen the scars on the hillsides and the badly eroded footpaths in popular walking areas that pay testament to that fact.

So is there anything that we can do to limit our impact on the countryside? Should we be burning our walking boots and investing in a sturdy flask to sip from while looking at pristine hills from the comfort of the car park?

Not according to organizations such as Treadsoftly, the Leave No Trace Center for Outdoor Ethics, or the British Trust for Conservation Volunteers (BTCV). They believe that minimal impact hillwalking is about understanding where you are and using your better

judgment, not about learning a set of rules. An enlightened hillwalker leaves a lighter footprint; and with a bit of background information, treading lightly will become second nature.

The problem

In the 1980s, large boulder fields on Snowdon in North Wales were cleared to shore up and drain the ever-widening path with rock-filled wire cages and concrete culverts. Elsewhere, the popularity of the Yorkshire Three Peaks meant that, on Pen-y-ghent, wooden planks were hammered into the hillside to build steps to the summit of this diminutive but rugged peak, in an experiment with erosion control.

These techniques are seen as being quite heavy-handed today. More consideration is given to building footpaths which are in keeping with the environment. Path-builders make use of locally sourced stone, which weathers better; and efforts are made to protect vegetation and replant with local species.

The path leading down Dollywagon Pike is the largest man-made scar in England's Lake District National Park. A footpath has been built to alleviate pressure on plants and grasses that hold the soil together, but their hard work is undone by people who either ignore the path altogether, or cut corners. This creates secondary paths which turn into water channels and can undermine the original paths.

The erosion scar on a prominent path in Langdale in the English Lake District grew to 120m (394ft) across and 3m (10ft) deep in places. Path diversions, replanting and the building of a pitched stone path have made the erosion much more manageable. Traditional pitched paths are suitable for packhorses, but unfortunately they make a difficult walking surface for us. So erosion gullies often form to the side of the path where people avoid the steep, sloping path. Modern pitched paths now favour staggered stone steps set at different heights. These are easier and safer to walk down, and that helps prevent erosion. Water

soon follows fresh tracks, causing damage and scarring the hillsides. So when you're walking along a footpath, ignore any existing short cuts and don't make new ones. The seconds you save can take years to mend.

Popular paths

When the Pennine Way became Britain's first official long-distance path in 1965, the route was set out along existing footpaths, old mine and drovers' tracks. Parts of the Way were suffering badly from erosion, and so flagstones from demolished Lancashire cotton mills were helicoptered out and laid on the fragile peat moorland to make a durable walking surface. These paths were built in the traditional 'causey' style. This path style is quite visible, but it does allow the surrounding vegetation to regenerate, and the flagstones are a reminder of the area's industrial heritage.

The solution

If the path divides, follow the path surface, and don't be tempted to walk to one side of it along the grass at the edge of the path. Trampled verges collapse, widening paths into broad, ugly scars. Go in single file where possible, because walking off the main path will widen the trail. When there are two tracks available to walk on, try to keep to the main path – even if it means getting muddy.

If you're faced with more than one possible path, it's considered best practice to walk on the beaten track. Careful walkers protect fragile and vulnerable paths, and avoid short cuts which damage vegetation and make the topsoil unstable. On steep terrain, short cuts quickly become channels for rainwater run-off, and can easily turn into deep erosion scars which can take many years to repair.

Switchbacks

If there are switchbacks, or zig-zags, built in to the path, use them. They're not just better for the vegetation, they're better for you. If you follow the most direct route of descent you get to the bottom marginally quicker, but you're putting much more strain on your knees.

Pathless terrain

However, when you're walking in more remote country across open ground, it's better to spread out as a group, keeping an eye out for ground nesting birds, rather than adopting single file, so that you don't trample the vegetation and create the beginnings of a path.

Cairns

There is a long-running debate about the value of cairns in mountain environments. Some believe that cairns are visually intrusive and unnecessary, particularly when built close to a

to damage. A stone on a path is a barrier against trampling; a stone on a cairn isn't doing anything useful.

Boggy ground

Squelchy, evil-smelling, sucking gloop – not exactly the most enticing walking surface, but one that's hard to avoid in the hills, especially on popular walk-in areas through moorland or a damp valley. If you think that the effect it has on your boots is bad, look behind at your footprints and you might be surprised to see the effect your boots have had on the ground. This is most obvious on paths running over level terrain. A path with lots of cover, whether it's in the form of vegetation or stones, allows rainwater to drain away underneath. However, as a path becomes trampled, the soil is packed firm and the rainwater can't drain away, so it collects, turning the surrounding ground into mud and bog.

If your path crosses a short, boggy section, the best thing is to take the shortest and most direct route through it, using any stones or logs that have been put there to step on. The most damaging way to cross boggy bits is to walk on the surrounding vegetation. You may think that, by avoiding the eroded section, you're not adding to the existing problem; but in fact, your 'environmental footprint' is smaller if you stick to the path, no matter how boggy it is. Several people walking around it will only make the problem bigger.

well-marked path. However, established cairns, such as those which mark an obscure junction, the start of a scramble or a given point on a summit plateau, play a very useful and widely accepted role in mountain navigation, and some old cairns are also of historical interest.

The cairn shown on the left was discovered by a National Park ranger, who did a double-take when he noticed that, overnight, a small and inconspicuous pile of stones had become a huge cairn. It was built from nothing, perhaps by a school group, but its presence by the side of an obvious path means that it has no useful purpose. Every stone on this cairn has been removed from the surrounding hillside.

Stones help to stabilize paths and provide a packed surface, protecting the vegetation and soil from heavy foot traffic, but in cairn form they're not doing that job.

Many of us were taught to add a stone as we passed a cairn, but now the practice is actively discouraged because it can trigger the erosion of the area around the cairn. When you remove a stone from the ground, you're open-ing up that piece of ground

is natural. This is where the earth is worn away by freeze-thawing or by water erosion and it becomes unstable. Walkers should avoid sitting on banks like this, as there's a tendency to prop feet up against the earth, cutting further into the bank and making it much more likely that the overhang will collapse.

Muck spreaders

There's nothing quite as unattractive as finding litter in the hills, and some supposedly biodegradable items will take longer than normal to break down when they are abandoned on a cold mountain summit. Degradability depends on climate and circumstances. Here is a rough guide to litter degradability:

- orange peel/banana skin: up to 2 years
- cigarette butts: up to 2 years
- plastic bags: 10 to 20 years
- tin cans: 50 years
- aluminium cans: between 80 and 100 years
- plastic mineral water bottles: indefinitely

Litter attracts litter. Walk up to the summit of any popular mountain and see how true that is. It's good not to drop litter, but it's even better to make a positive contribution to the environment by picking up other people's rubbish as you head home. Get into the habit

Trekking poles

Some popular trails have three sets of tracks: one made by feet, and one narrower track either side made by trekking poles. Their impact is greatest on flat, boggy ground. This is where you need to make a judgment – do I really need my trekking poles here? Will they damage this terrain? For example, peaty paths are vulnerable to erosion; so, if you're walking on the flat on peaty ground, consider stowing your poles away until you get to the ascents or descents, because this is where you'll get most benefit from them.

Scree-running

When you're descending over stony ground, place your feet deliberately and carefully, rather than relying on momentum to keep you upright. Scree-running is fun, but it displaces huge amounts of protective surface material from the hillside to the bottom of the hill, and leads to worse erosion. Scree can be 'planted' to stabilize the slope again, so it's not irreversible. However, this is a big job and it's far better to avoid these problems by careful walking.

Overhanging banks

Some erosion, such as on overhanging grassy banks,

of carrying a designated rubbish bag in your rucksack (for your own trash, at least) so your spare fleece doesn't get covered in soggy banana skin.

And finally...

Human waste can ruin an area, so it's important to plan your 'natural breaks' sensitively around three principles. Make sure that (i) it won't be 'discovered' by anyone else (at least 50m/yd from the path, and not in enclosed spaces such as caves, ruined buildings or behind huts); (ii) it's not going to pollute water (30m/yd from streams), and (iii) it is somewhere it can break down quickly. If you dig a hole, mix it with soil, fill in the hole and camouflage the surface. Burn toilet paper, rather than burying it, but if there's any fire risk, bag up your bog roll and take it home.

Useful addresses

Britain and Europe

British Mountaineering Council
177–179 Burton Road
Manchester M20 2BB,
Tel: 0870 010 4878
Fax: 0161 445 4500
Email: office@thebmc.co.uk
Website: www.thebmc.co.uk

Mountaineering Council of Ireland
Sport HQ, 13 Joyce Way
Parkwest Business Park
Dublin 12
Tel: 1 625 1115
Fax: 1 625 1116
Email mci@eircom.net
Website: www.mountaineering.ie

The Mountaineering Council of Scotland
The Old Granary
West Mill St, Perth PH1 5QP
Tel:. 01738 638227
Fax. 01738 442095
Email: info@mountaineering-scotland.org.uk
Website: www.mountaineering-scotland.org.uk

Ramblers' Association
2nd Floor Camelford House
87-90 Albert Embankment
London SE1 7TW
Tel: 020 7339 8500
Fax: 020 7339 8501
Email: ramblers@london.ramblers.org.uk
Website: www.ramblers.org.uk

Mountain Bothies Association
Website: www.mountainbothies.org.uk

British Red Cross
First aid training
Website: www.redcross.co.uk

Union Internationale des Associations d'Alpinisme (UIAA)
Monbijoustrasse 61 Postfach
CH-3000 Bern 23
Switzerland
Tel: (0)31 370 1828
Fax: (0)31 370 1838
Email: office@uiaa.ch
Website: www.uiaa.ch

Trail Magazine
Website: www.trailroutes.com;
www.greatmagazines.co.uk

North America

The Alpine Club of Canada
PO Box 8040, Indian Flats Road
Canmore, Alberta T1W 2T8
Tel: 403 678 3200
Fax: 403 678 3224
Email info@alpineclubofcanada.ca
Website: www.alpinclubofcanada.ca

Appalachian Mountain Club
Main Office, 5 Joy Street
Boston, MA 02108
Tel: (617) 523 0636
Fax: (617) 523 0722
Email: information@outdoors.org
Website: www.outdoors.org

Leave No Trace Center for Outdoor Ethics
PO Box 997
Boulder, Colorado CO 80306
Tel: (303) 442 8222
Fax: (303) 442 8217
Website: www.lnt.org

The Mountaineers
300 Third Avenue West
Seattle, Washington WA 98119
Tel: (206) 284 6310
Fax: (206) 284 4977
Email: clubmail@mountaineers.org
Website: www.mountaineers.org

National Outdoor Leadership School (NOLS)
284 Lincoln Street, Lander
Wyoming WY 82520-2848
Tel: (800) 710 6657
Fax: (307) 332 1220
Email: admissions@nols.edu
Website: www.nols.edu

National Park Service (US)
1849 C Street NW
Washington DC 20240
Tel: (202) 208-6843
Website: www.nps.gov

Red Cross First Aid Training
USA website: www.redcross.org
Canada website: www.redcross.ca

Australia and New Zealand

Bushwalking Australia
PO Box 6067, Linden Park
Adelaide, SA 5065
Email: office@walkingsa.org.au
Website: www.bushwalkingaustralia.org

Federated Mountain Clubs of New Zealand (FMC)
PO Box 1604, Wellington
Tel: (0)4 233 8244
Email: fmcsec@xtra.co.nz
Website: fmc.org.nz

New Zealand Mountain Safety Council
3rd Floor Mountain Safety House
19 Tory Street, Wellington
Phone: 4 385 7162
Fax: 4 385 7366
Email: info@mountainsafety.org.nz
Website: www.mountainsafety.org.nz

Red Cross First Aid Training
Australia website: www.redcross.org.au
New Zealand website:
www.redcross.org.nz

Index